Solo

'83 /85

662

LIT. Bio.

For those who may have wondered
if I ever got there

Solo

One

On a serene and dazzling California morning, the air fragrant with orange blossoms, the light shimmering and misty with the smoke of sprinklers, I left the sheltered halls of learning for a *Wanderjahr* in Europe. I had kissed a few girls, and had read a few books, including *The Decline of the West,* by Oswald Spengler, to whom I had written to question his assumption that the West had declined west of the Missouri River. Of east of the Missouri I hesitated to speak, but of the west I had personal experience. To this letter he had not replied, but perhaps he needed time to think it over. If and when I was in or near Munich I would look him up.

I may have felt that college life had softened me up, since I planned to hitchhike to Chicago and spend the summer working at the 1933 Century of Progress, a world's fair. A fraternity brother had offered me a job at the Schlitz Garden Café on the island. With my nest egg enlarged, I would proceed to New York and work my passage on a cattle boat to France, a hot tip I had picked up from Richard Halliburton, world traveler and author of *The Royal Road to Romance*. I also had the name of a man, with fraternity connections, last believed to be living in a garret in Paris, and the address of a woman of some mystery, thought to be at home in Mallorca. I was not without experience, of an artless sort, but I had yet to ride the rails, spend the night in a hoosegow or sit around the smoking fire in a hobo jungle, swapping yarns and the butts of cigarettes, all known to be indispensable in the education of an American writer. As the author of

> *The sun*
> *Sweats through the fog*

I was not without a show of style and substance.

One of my professors drove me as far as Provo, Utah, from where I made my way eastward toward Colorado. Clear and sparkling mountain water purled in the roadside ditches, but there was little but local eastbound traffic. I had failed to consider that late in May the snow still blocked some of the mountain passes. Just east of Vernal, I spent the long morning at the side of the road, waiting. In the glare of high noon, I stepped from the shade to watch a car slowly approach. It passed me without raising dust from the gravel road. The two farmers seated in the front looked at me, the younger man firmly gripping the vibrating wheel. Down the road fifty yards or so, the car pulled over and stopped. When I came alongside, both men studied me through the buzz of flies traveling with them.

"Can you read?" one asked me. I said I could read. He reached to open the rear door for me, and I climbed in. We then cruised along for two or three miles in the car's second gear. "He says he can read," he said to his companion. From the brown bag he clutched in his lap the older man removed a wrapped bottle of Listerine. As he handed it to me, he said, "Read it out loud."

I read aloud the directions printed on the green wrapper, including the fine print. All that they heard seemed to reassure them. They glanced at each other, then the younger one said that if I wouldn't mind waiting, while they tended to a sick horse, they would give me a lift as far as the Green River, about twelve miles. I said I wouldn't mind.

A mile or so ahead, the car left the highway to follow a narrow dirt trail to the top of a barren rise. In the blazing noon light the dilapidated buildings cast deep, vibrant shadows. When the car's motor stopped I could hear the hornet-like drone of the flies. In the yard, hard and smooth as a floor, a big horse stood near the tilted barn in a cloud of flies, a fly net draped over his body. He didn't trouble to twitch his hide or switch his tail. Three or four barefooted kids, the same color as the yard, sat in the shadow of the house without moving or speaking. I had never seen kids that age so quiet. The man with the bottle of mouthwash peeled off the wrapper and used the blade of his pocket knife to pry out the cork. Both men had a good sniff of it. One of them poured some of the liquid into his palm and slapped it on the rump of the horse, like a shaving lotion. He did that four or five times, until the black pelt glistened, then he stepped back to wait for the horse to feel better. The sweet smell of the mouthwash seemed to increase the drone of the flies. The big horse just stood there, like a propped barrel, his head hung low as if he was asleep on his feet. It seemed to me his rear quarters looked swollen.

"What's the matter with him?" I asked.

One said, "He's been gelded, but he don't get better."

Once more the man slapped the horse with the mouthwash, then he spoke to him in a comforting manner. The horse's name was Tom. The other one picked up a piece of plank from the yard and thumped the horse across the backside with it. "He's got to move around," he said. "We got to move him." The one with the bottle went to the front of the horse and gave a tug on the bridle, but nothing would budge him. Through the cloud of flies over the horse's rump the side of the barn shimmered with heat. "Get going, Tom," one yelled, and gave him another loud whack with the board.

Not feeling so good, I moved to stand in the shade of the barn. Through the window at the back of the house

I could hear a woman's voice singing hymns. I noticed a brown-and-white dog lying under the car as if he was dead. I thought I might pass out if I just stood there, listening to the drone of the flies and the whack of the board, so I crossed the yard and went down the driveway without anybody speaking to me. When I got to the road I sprawled out in the ditch grass, my face in the cool dampness at its roots. I just lay there till I felt better, as hot as it was. Now and then I could hear one of the louder whacks on the horse's rump. No one called to me, and it led me to think that whatever ailed the horse might ail all of them, and that they needed more than mouth-wash.

A mile or so down the road, feeling a little better, I wondered how much of what I had seen had actually been there and how much the heat and flies had led me to imagine. In either case, it was the sort of experience I valued, but I seemed to lack the stomach for it. The stomach would come, I told myself, when I had toughened up.

In the ten or twelve miles I walked to the Green River, my shadow lengthened before me, but no car passed in either direction. There was more traffic to the north, across Wyoming, and to the south, across New Mexico, but I had previously detoured around the Rockies and I was determined to pass through them. Four days later I was still in Jensen City, on the Green River, where a road crew was working on the bridge. From one of these men I heard that dinosaurs had left their tracks in the rocks to the north. Lucky for me, I was not one of those green-horns who believed everything they heard. Not far up the river, where I could see his fire at night, a white-bearded prospector camped with his burro, eating cold beans from a can with the blade of his bowie knife. He did cook the bacon he cut from a slab, however, and shared with me the coffee he boiled in a Crisco can. I shared with him one of my Camel cigarettes.

Having once vowed not to smoke until I was twenty-one (for which I had received, and wore, a skull and crossbones medal), at twenty-three I was free of that vow but not to the extent of freely inhaling. I was saving myself. In practical terms, it added up to a lot of cigarettes.

A schoolteacher and his wife, from Pocatello, Idaho, gave me a ride over the mountains to Greeley, Colorado, with a stop along the way at Steamboat Springs, but from Greeley it took me almost two days to hitch the hundred miles or so to Sterling, a railroad town on the South Platte. I could have taken a bus from there as far as North Platte, Nebraska, where there would be more eastbound traffic, but in all my previous cross-country travel, the one thing I hadn't done was ride the rails. It scared me to think about it: but not to face up to it scared me worse.

Just at sunset, concealed like Brer Rabbit in the bushes and shrubs near the station, I saw the headlight of an eastbound freight locomotive far down the tracks, smoking like a comet. As it approached, the earth trembled. I waited till the cars were clattering in the railyard, and

I could see the insignia, like coats of arms, painted on the black metal of the tank cars—the Denver & Rio Grande, the Missouri Pacific, the Chicago, Burlington & Quincy, the Atchison, Topeka & Santa Fe—the first, and lasting, exposure I had had to the open and royal road to romance. But until I ran, hooting, from the shadows, I had had no idea there were a dozen or so like me crouched there, now all running for dear life and hooting like savages. One ahead of me stumbled and fell, another came up and ran by me, although in my panic I surely ran faster than I might have, until the clamor of the freight cars, right there at my side, proved to be an adversary I could compete with. I managed to get a firm grip on a rung of a ladder and climb to the top of a car. Luckily, I had picked one with an ice hatch open, and I could see the pale faces in the gloom below me. The boy who followed me down closed the hatch and there we all were, invisible in the darkness. As the freight picked up speed, the awful racket made it impossible to talk. A few matches flickered, cigarettes glowed. Where, I wondered, were we headed? In the freightyards the cars might be shifted around and go north to South Dakota, or south to Kansas. I was hoping to go eastward along the broad Platte valley through such towns as Kearney, Grand Island and Central City. I had lived in them all. In Central City I had been born. That had meant little to me until the prospect of seeing it again from the top of a freight car, clattering through it downgrade just about sunrise. In the slanting light of sunrise I could see all the way from Central City to Chapman, from one

7

grain elevator to another. In a tassel-fringed buggy, the horse's tail sweeping the buckboard, my father had driven me all the way to Grand Island, more than twenty-five miles, to have my adenoids out. From the tops of freight cars parked near the grain elevator I had had my first bird's-eye view of Central City, and was able to fathom, for the first time, the disorderly pattern of its streets. Part of the town, *my* part, paralleled the Union Pacific, and part of it paralleled the Lincoln Highway, which entered town from the east but left it headed southwest. This resulted in a public square with a dog leg, and streets that entered and left from every point of the compass. I would see all of that again, and more, if I was seated atop a freight car and we passed through the town after daylight.

When the first light appeared at the cracks in the hatch I climbed out of the compartment to ride on the top. Where were we? I had no idea. Dawn light dimly revealed the flat Platte valley. The empty freight clattered down the grade like a runaway train. Every ten or twenty minutes we flashed through a town with its water tank and grain elevator, the cattle loader on a siding across from the station. Cinders and smoke streamed into my face from the black plume of the locomotive. I lay out flat, straining to read the names on the water tanks and grain elevators. The big town of Grand Island alerted me that Chapman was up ahead, what little there was of it, with the cemetery where my mother lay buried. East of Chapman, veiled by the smoke, and much less imposing than I remembered, a black water stack rose from a clump of trees, concealing the station where my father had been the agent. Just beyond it the crossing gates had been lowered, the clanging bell changing its pitch as we thundered past. A mile to the north, where the Burlington locomotive with its big funnel stack made its approach to the town, my father had attempted to raise leghorn chickens and sell day-old eggs to the dining car service. In an upstairs bedroom of the farmhouse, where they played records on her new Victrola, his pretty wife of one year and his nine-year-old son, recently freed of his adenoids, watched from the window as the leghorns died and were buried in deep pits of quicklime. What did that have to do with the young man on the freight car, traveling eastward into the future? I turned to watch it all recede behind me and vanish like smoke: switch tower, grain elevator, water stack, the station where my father had sat, fingering the ticker or looking off to where the tracks blurred on the horizon. Racing into the future, I saw it all vanish, and felt only relief.

My passage through the landscape on the top of a freight car corresponded to my passage as a child, when I perceived, through shuttered chinks of time, the cloudy happenings I would one day transform into fictions. The sleeping town was in the grip of the Depression, a clump of faded green in the surrounding dust bowl, but I would not see that until a year later, when I was headed back to California. Hardly a whisper of all that had reached me between the pages of Spengler and Halliburton, whose opposing views—from the top of the freight car— awaited my firsthand confirmation. For a youth from a landscape so empty it awaited settlement by figures of the imagination, the high road of romance was the one to take atop a swaying Missouri Pacific fruit car. I would note that later, on my arrival in Omaha.

Two

I spent the summer, and it seemed a long one, in the Schlitz Garden Café at the Century of Progress. I rose from thirteen dollars a week, plus my food, to eighteen dollars a week by the first of October, at which time I quit. My nest egg had grown to $360, which I figured would last me a year if I managed to live on a dollar a day. I had a new gabardine suit, a pair of crepe-soled shoes, a Schick razor with a year's supply of blades in the handle, an extra shirt, a change of socks, a Parker pen, a notebook, and a Modern Library edition of Thomas Mann's *The Magic Mountain*. I had already read it, but it would seem a different book if I read it at sea, on a cattle boat.

In New York I took a room at the Sloane House YMCA, and spent a week walking the waterfront, looking for a cattle boat. No one I spoke to had ever seen cattle on a boat. It was costing me two dollars a day to live in New York, so I paid for a passage on the *Black Gull,* a freighter sailing from Weehawken to Antwerp. When I got over to Weehawken, where it was docked, the boat looked pretty small. Sol Yellig, a passenger, was there before I was, and we had all day to look the boat over. Sol was from Brooklyn, on his way to Russia, where his father had an investment in the future as an engineer. The two others in my cabin included a Swede, named Lindstrom, and Mr. Schutzel, or Schlussel (I never knew which), who had been a janitor in Des Moines and was now going home to Austria. In his twenty-eight years in Des Moines, Mr. Schutzel had not learned much English. He was a stocky man, very short in the leg, his blue serge suit as shiny as oilcloth; the pants proved to be worn so thin at the knees his underwear showed through when he was seated.

Sven Lindstrom was an artist, on his way to his home in Oslo, having overstayed his student visa. He had all his stuff in a duffel, like a sailor, but he carried his guitar in a black wooden case. Until the boat sailed, he stayed belowdecks, plucking the strings and singing Russian folk songs. There were two other cabins, one with four people, and a small cabin with two people on their honeymoon, Mr. and Mrs. Lennox from Enid, Oklahoma. We were all out on the deck, even Mr. Lindstrom, when we finally embarked and sailed down the river. As we passed the Statue of Liberty, Sol Yellig turned to me and said, "What a joke."

That startled me at the time, but I reasoned it might be the way that the smart-alecky types from Brooklyn saw it. I had now seen the Pacific, and swum in it, and in a few hours I would be crossing the Atlantic, and in the spring, or maybe even sooner, I would gaze on the blue Mediterranean. Lord Byron might have ruined the isles of Greece for me, being a bit too romantic for my taste.

The *Black Gull* had a full cargo, and set low in the sea. I liked that when I stood along the rail or up at the bow, where the spray would drench me. At the boat's midsection, around the covered hold, there was room to walk up and down and space for a few folding chairs. The honeymoon couple usually got two of them, and Mr. Siegfried Liszt was usually in the other, since it was his custom to be up about daylight. Mr. Liszt had been a chief clerk at a bank in New York but he now planned to study medicine in Vienna, where he was from. His mother still lived there, in suburban Vienna, just across from what had been his father's wagon wheel factory, the name s. z. LISZT still visible on the bricks in the photograph he showed me. With the rise of the automobile, of course, the wagon wheel business had not been so good.

The food was all right and there was plenty of it, but getting in and out of the small dining room across from the galley proved to be a problem. The table filled the room so tightly there was not enough space to squeeze behind the chairs when getting in and out. The smart and fast eaters soon sat near the door, with the slow and big eaters at the back. Another thing we learned to do was take the food at the door, handed across from the

13

galley, and then pass it around the table so no one had to serve it. After dinner some of us would sit there and play cards and dominoes, while the others talked.

In the talk it turned out that Mr. Liszt had once been a student of literature in Vienna, a reader of Oswald Spengler and Thomas Mann. It saddened him to hear that I was reading *The Magic Mountain,* since so much of it was lost in the translation. If I so desired it, he would restore for me much that had been lost. I so desired it, but the wind on the deck made it hard to discuss such serious matters, and if we sat inside with the others, we had trouble with Dr. Haffner. Dr. Haffner was a year younger than I was, but he already had his own practice in Milwaukee and was on his way for a year of study in Stuttgart. He was a heavy-set young man, very tight in his checkered suit, with short, pudgy fingers and a round baby face. He spent most of his time reading medical journals and helping the young married couple with their French. To show me the subtleties involved in translation, Mr. Liszt read aloud to me from his copy of Count Keyserling's *Travel Diary.* The moment he would translate what he had read, Dr. Haffner would snort, like stifling a sneeze, or wag his head from side to side as if it pained him. On occasion he would blurt out something that I understood without the need of translation. *Dummkopf,* for example, I figured out for myself.

Mr. Liszt soon came to feel, in the privacy of his cabin, that a young scholar like myself, with my love of German literature, might find Vienna more attractive than Paris. For one thing, the living would be much cheaper, and for another, the Viennese were more *gemütlich*. And what was *gemütlich*? Dr. Haffner, on hearing this word, had blown a sound through his lips that required no translation. Mr. Liszt remained silent, his own red lips puckered, his hands smoothing the wrinkles from his napkin. After a few days in Paris, he said, I would be able to appreciate what was *gemütlich* about Vienna. The people were more friendly and easygoing. The language itself— if he might say so—would prove easier to master, for the French were particularly scornful of beginners. The young married couple, in Mr. Liszt's opinion, were due for a rude awakening. In Vienna, in contrast, I would find people eager to be helpful—especially young women. Mr. Liszt spoke respectfully of Viennese women, but not without a flush that reddened his neck and ears. He was up so early, to occupy a folding chair, his freshly shaved jowls dusted with talcum, that by early afternoon his face looked blue with a five-o'clock shadow. Until I met Mr. Liszt and Dr. Haffner, and had some long talks with Sol Yellig, I thought there had to be something special between people who spoke the same language. I found that there was. The dislike they had for each other was more refined than that for people in general.

Dr. Haffner was really a *Wunderkind*, Mr. Liszt advised me, who knew all about poison gas, bugs and germ warfare, and it had come to his attention that he sent wireless messages to Berlin and Hamburg. Had I also noticed that Dr. Haffner never missed the German broadcasts of Hitler? I had heard one myself, the hoarse voice of the Führer lifted and blowing on the roars of those who were listening, but the static was so bad Mr. Liszt couldn't tell me much that he had said. The message I got was not one a translation would have helped.

My cabinmate Sven Lindstrom liked to sit on his upper bunk with his bare legs dangling and sing *"Ochy Chornia."* Sol Yellig liked to sing along with him. Anything to do with Russia he thought was wonderful. He had never been there, but he knew that Russian women were wonderful. I had had a weakness for Russia myself and might have planned to go there if it had been nearer, but after five days and nights with Sol Yellig I knew I could live without it. The likable side of Sol was apparent when you caught him at something, which wasn't at all hard, and he would smile and shrug.

I often saw the honeymoon couple up at the bow of the boat, but seldom up close. If the boat was rocking he would grip the rail so she could stand with one arm around him, the other holding the book she was reading. I was curious about what the book was, but it had a plain lending library jacket. If they were in the lounge, and I spoke to one of them, she always did the talking. She was nice, but one of those tall, gangly women it wouldn't have crossed my mind to marry. After several days at sea he began a beard, which grew in orange like the coloring that came with margarine, so he shaved it off.

Near the mid-Atlantic we had some bad weather, with seas so high they spilled into the gangway. Sol Yellig was sick, Mr. Liszt was sick, and the honeymoon couple in particular were sick, but Mr. Schutzel, Lindstrom and the *Wunderkind* didn't miss a meal. I wasn't *really* sick, but the

16

thought of food made me stand in the gangway, the spray in my face, breathing in deeply until I felt better. What I wanted to know, and had a chance to find out, was the difference between a real storm at sea and reading about a storm in Conrad. When I came to know the difference, however, and the sea had calmed, it was Conrad's storm that I remembered.

We were anchored in the pea-soup fog of the Channel for the thirteenth and fourteenth day of our crossing, and on the sixteenth of October, at about three in the morning, we made our way up the Schelde to Antwerp. I could see, hanging out of the fog, the telephone wires, as though they were all dangling from a maypole, and in the street along the dock the cobblestones glistened like metal. Not a sound anywhere. When the gangplank was lowered, clattering like a drawbridge, every window in a building I had thought might be empty went up as if a fire alarm had sounded. Framed in the windows, in nothing but their nightshirts, were the wonderful whores Sven had been telling us about. Some were leaning out and hooting, a racket like none I had ever heard. While I was on the deck, leaning over the rail, Sven ran down the gangplank in his pajamas, then ran the full length of the street, waving and throwing kisses, as if uncertain which one of them to choose. I can describe it, but who would ever believe it? The fatter women leaned from the windows holding their breasts in their hands. Sven didn't seem to notice any more than I did the car that came out of nowhere and moved up behind him. Two big fellows picked him up, the way you would a kid, put him into the car and drove off. Some of the women continued to hoot and wave—there were eight or ten of us out on the deck —but when we just stood there staring, doing nothing, they slammed down their windows and went back to bed. It was suddenly so quiet we could hear drops of water drip from the wires. If nothing else had happened to me in Europe, I would have felt that what I had seen was well worth the trouble, but when I was safely back in the cabin it shamed me to see that Sven's bunk was empty. His guitar was still there, and his bag was unpacked. It had never crossed my mind that he would have the nerve to act as good as he talked. "I'm going to get me five women," he had said, "and go to bed for a week." I would have personally settled for one *good* woman, but when the time came, and he set an example, I stood on the deck with all the other chickens. I also agreed with them all that he was either crazy or a sex maniac. At times I thought I might be both, but here I was on my first night in the old world, with a whole year of it before me, and it scared me to think that I might catch something and not be able to do anything about it. Not on a dollar a day. The fact is, since I had to miss something, I wouldn't have missed what I had just seen. That's what I told myself.

I spent the day in Antwerp avoiding Sol Yellig and the honeymoon couple, who turned up all over. On the night train to Paris I shared the compartment with two peasant women, wrapped up in their shawls like parcels, each one with a fat goose in her lap. The women dozed off, but the geese and I kept wary eyes on each other. I'd been up since three in the morning, and all day on my feet, but if I let myself sleep I might miss something.

I managed to stay awake by standing in the aisle, letting the night air blow into my face. In the early dawn light I saw the fields of France, some with rows of stubble and the big two-wheeled carts I had seen in Van Gogh's paintings. It seemed normal to me that most of what I saw far exceeded my expectations. Wasn't it for this I had come to Europe? In the Gare St. Lazare my excitement was so great I watched people eating croissants and forgot to eat myself. The people milling around were smaller than I had expected and showed no interest in me whatsoever. That was surprising. In America I would have shown real interest in them. The way the waiters stood at the front of the sidewalk cafés, flipping their cloths at the chair seats, kept me from sitting down. At a busy intersection, the air blue with the exhausts of the buses, I saw a classmate of mine I had never much liked sitting on a bench at a bus stop. He had been a senior, a class ahead of me, who always wore a coat and tie to his classes. Here in Paris he wore a topcoat, with the collar turned up, and a rolled-brim fedora like those worn by my father. So far as I knew, he didn't write, or paint, or read the sort of books that were written in Paris, but on one occasion, because he had a car, I had got him a blind date. She was a smart girl and a good dancer, but after the dance she wouldn't get back in the rumble seat with him. She rode with us in the front. Later I asked him what had gone wrong.

"What I wanted was a real woman," he told me. "What you got me was a smart-ass schoolgirl."

If he had been a year in Paris I might have learned something from him, and we might even have had some good times together, but a person like that would naturally think that I had come to Paris for the same reason he did. I already had a woman. There would be two letters from her waiting for me at the American Express.

In the doorway of a shop I saw a girl who made me think of my girl, the way she was standing, looking at me over her shoulder, but when she smiled she had this one tooth, like a black kernel of corn, right in the middle of her uppers. When I smiled at her she made a gesture with her finger that was new to me, but not hard to understand.

I could read a little French, but what I heard all around me was like a language played backward. If I asked directions I never understood what was said. In the Luxembourg Gardens I sat on a bench listening to the cries and shouts of the children. One ran to stand before me, screaming like a parrot, shouting the same words until she was hoarse. Only when she ran off, and it was relatively quiet, did I realize she had been yelling, *"Me voici! Me voici!"* just like a small kid anywhere. But whatever people say in a language you don't understand seems interesting. Anxious to know what a real French apple tasted like, I bought two from a peddler, about the size of golf balls, but both had worms in them.

A classmate of mine had given me the address of a pension, near the Place St. Germaine, but when I spoke to the concierge at the door I could hear girls speaking English while they played Ping-Pong. Most of the time the ball just bounced around on the floor.

I got a room for the night near the Sorbonne, where a bird flew in and out of the small barred window. No one had told me that the toilets did not have bowls, where you could sit, but were like urinals and you had to crouch. The next two days it drizzled and all of Paris looked to me like one big dirty puddle. I decided it wasn't the right time of year for Paris and took the night train to Vienna, where the weather couldn't be any worse and the people might be more *gemütlich*. At the stop in Basel, the waitress in the station understood what I ordered, slipped me a second pat of butter, and wished me a *sehr glückliche Reise*. Thanks to her, that was what I was on, but at least I knew better than to try to tell her. *"Auf Wiedersehen,"* I said.

Three

On Kärntnerstrasse, near the Stephansdom, which Mr. Liszt had pointed out to me, we sat in a *Kaffeehaus* drinking large cups of coffee topped with whipped cream. When we arrived he had asked the waiter for a newspaper and it was brought to him. There were four or five old men in the café, all of them reading newspapers, but they looked a little drab and shabby compared to Mr. Liszt. His American suit had been pressed, and I could smell his aftershave lotion. I was very glad to see him, and he was friendly, but since I had last seen him on the boat he had changed. He was no longer the clerk in a New York bank, but a professor advising one of his students. His new reversible raincoat, with the tweed lining showing, hung on a hook with his plaid muffler tucked into the sleeve. My raincoat was so light that I sat with it on, my clothes still mussed from the night I had spent on the train.

We were seated, Mr. Liszt advised me, in a very famous *Kaffeehaus,* where many celebrated people had sat and talked, but to be perfectly frank, he seldom came here because the coffee was so expensive. I could believe that. Only Mrs. Mulligan's matchless eggnogs, in my Omaha boyhood, seemed to me at all comparable. I quickly said I would be glad to pay for my own, and he replied he had been about to suggest that. In the future, when we met in this manner, we would go *dutch.* Having the appropriate word for it made it acceptable to both of us.

He read the news in the paper, most of which was bad, then he made note of the rooms for rent that he considered inexpensive and suitable. There were several not far from the university, on the Ring. They were not nearby, but while we were walking he would point out the sights of interest. Near the Votivkirche was the Bankverein, where I would go to cash my traveler's checks. We stopped to buy some stamps at one of the kiosks, which also sold tobacco. Cigarettes could be bought one at a time, and we each bought one.

The first room we looked at was up three flights of stairs, where we found three women sitting in the kitchen, near a stove. They were greatly impressed by Mr. Liszt, who gave a little speech about my background, a scholar who had come all the way from California to study German literature in Vienna. They were dumbfounded, but so bundled up in shawls I saw little of their faces. The one who moved about the kitchen, and

showed us the room, wore skirts so long they swept the
floor. The room was right off the kitchen, with a bed, a
chair and a desk with a lamp. A large white bowl and
pitcher sat on a stand near the window. The room would
be warm, being so close to the kitchen, but Mr. Liszt
pointed out that to get in and out I would always be
passing through the room where the women were gathered.

We saw another one like it, but much darker, with a
wall blocking the light at the window, then we climbed
four flights of wide stairs to an apartment on the top
floor. A gray-haired woman with the eyes of a Gypsy, her
earrings swinging, peered at us through the crack in the
door. Shrilly we were welcomed, the hall floor gleaming
from the sweep of her skirts. A dim bulb glowed in the
dark hallway, but the room at the end of it was flooded
with light. The ceiling was high, as was the bed on which
she sat to show it was springy; there was a desk with
pigeonholes, a cold blue-tile stove, a white bowl and
pitcher on a marble-topped washstand. This room, with
Frühstück, of *Butterbrot* and *Schokolade,* came to about sixteen dollars a month. I liked both the room and the
gnädige Frau, who hustled about like the woman on the
can of Dutch Cleanser. Her name was Frau Unger. She
herself had come from Pest, across the Danube from
Buda. Her son Hermann, who loved to travel, had once
gone there on a river excursion. While his animated
mother opened wide the casement window to wave her
arms at the view and the gray roofs of Vienna, her son
Hermann, dressed in the coat and pants left him by his

father, an "official," stood patiently beside the stove, snapping the links of his cuffs, waiting to be introduced.

At eight in the morning Frau Unger would appear with my tray of *Butterbrot* and *Schokolade*. The thick slice of bread was dark and heavy, cut from a large round loaf in the delicatessen, and sold by the weight. The butter moist and unsalted. The chocolate rich and sweet. After asking me how well I had slept, she would stand, her hands rolled up in her apron, watching me eat. It seemed to astonish her that a youth who had come from where I did knew how to do it.

Was the bed soft?

Jawohl!

Was the food good?

Jawohl!

When she heard me say *jawohl,* her eyes flashed, her head wagged with pleasure, rocking her earrings. Her lips parted expectantly on her gold-capped teeth. What a woman Herr Unger had found himself before he died in the Great War. She was tall, with wide hips, and listened to me with her head cocked, like a worming robin. She contrived many ways to conceal her hands, with the knobby knuckles, but there was always something that required doing. In Vienna the beds came with a feather mattress that one slept on, and another that one slept beneath. Both of these had to be aired at the open window, where they were shaken and given a good pummeling. The high window seemed to frame most of the roofs in Vienna, but nothing in the way of a landmark. Occasionally I saw the sun shining elsewhere, but never on my window. After several years of living in Southern California, I found the fall air of Vienna cold. It was early November. In the garden directly below the window, the bushes and the shrubs were bare. Gravel paths, with crisp right angles, divided the garden into sections, each with a bench like those in a park. One morning I had seen a couple seated on a bench, the woman with her hands in a fur muff, the man with his chin resting on his cane.

While my bed and the room were being aired, I wore my raincoat as a bathrobe. After breakfast I would walk up and down conjugating German verbs until Frau Unger's son Hermann paid me a social visit. He was small and frail, not at all like his mother, except for the teeth that kept his lips from closing. Hermann's large rabbit eyes were warm and gentle, and his nostrils, like those of a girl I had known, quivered in moments of excitement. He had inherited all of his clothes from his father, in the style that was current before the war. I had never before actually known a young man who wore spats. They were mouse-colored, with pearl buttons on the side, and he had several pairs. When he came to see me, snapping the links on his cuffs as he bowed, I was part of a movie of social high life, starring Bebe Daniels and Adolphe Menjou. Hermann had been born while the Hapsburgs were still in power. He told me this as we stood at the window, the pupils of his eyes as pale as water. Hapsburg was a name that meant as much to him as Jefferson and Washington meant to me, and I noticed that in the excitement of his recitation his gums tended to bleed, staining his teeth. In the strong light at the window, his pupils narrowed like a cat's. When he extended his arm to point into the garden, I noticed that his cuffs were not part of a shirt but fastened with pins to the sleeve of his jacket. It shamed me to see these details so clearly, but that did not stop me from looking. I marveled how, with a head so small, he had such a snow of dandruff on his collar. When he smiled at me, the tip of his tongue wiped the pink stain from his teeth.

Hermann had studied English, like his father, and he now wrote business letters, in English, for a bicycle firm on Florianigasse, all of which he signed "Your Obedient Humble Servant." If I would speak English and correct his grammar, he would speak and correct my German. At my suggestion he brought in a chair, on which, after bowing, he would sit. In this way the young American in his raincoat and Hermann Unger of the Hapsburg Empire would discuss the weather or New York City (*wunderbar, fabelhaft, grossartig,* etc.) while smoking short tubes of paper into which had been stuffed something like excelsior. Hermann made them himself every morning, on a machine with a crank. When he departed he bowed, taking the chair with him, then discussed all that had been said with Frau Unger, whose laugh was shrill, her voice loud and penetrating.

If I pause here to consider what I have just written, to what extent is it true to what I remember? To what extent is what I remember true to Hermann? He stood near the door, on entering the room, until I actually beckoned him closer. He was at once very eager to talk and reluctant, as if he privately had his doubts that he was the person he appeared to be in public. I liked him. This may have been at the heart of what I liked.

I would work for an hour or more on German verbs and vocabulary, then walk down Florianigasse, a street with many zigs and zags, to the university on the Ringstrasse. The school was in operation but the halls seemed empty. I had inquired about courses in German for beginners, and been advised to join the Foreign Students Club, on Schottengasse. The club had its rooms on the second floor of a building directly across the street from the bank. One of the rooms had several chairs, a rack of newspapers, a fireplace where people without chairs could stand and talk. A large adjoining room, without a rug, had a billiard table, a rack with cues on the wall, and two smaller tables for checkers and chess. At twelve o'clock and at six, the club served meals for as little as one schilling, about twenty-five cents. If I was careful and frugal, I could live through the winter on thirty dollars a month, a sum I could afford.

All foreigners, especially those speaking English, were in demand for the exchange conversations with both native and other foreign students. Whether the American language was English or not was one of our topics of discussion. The Finns, who proved to be pretty clannish, took over the billiard table in the morning, then let the Czechs have it in the afternoon. At least four or five young men were British, and spoke the much admired Oxford English, the vowels so broad and nasal I missed a good deal that they were saying. I was not the only American—there was a girl from Buffalo and one from Brooklyn, and a graduate student from Yale who did not feel the two of us had much in common. In theory, at least, an hour's exchange conversation would give each person half an hour to listen and half an hour to talk, but in practice, as I soon found out, I spent about forty-five minutes listening. Those experienced with exchange conversations, and there were many of them, knew how to make the most out of every discussion. And how are you, Herr Morris? *Sehr gut,* says I. And then he or she tells me, for most of the hour, how he or she is, in great detail.

On the plus side, it did mean that I was very popular. There was little I could say in German, but I proved to be a good listener. Five students signed up to converse with me, including a young woman physical education instructor—phys ed was very popular in Vienna—with a Swiss fiancé in Poughkeepsie. Twice a week I met with her in the alcove of the game room, where we would sit at one of the windows. Her face was still tanned from a summer of mountain climbing, her shoulders were broad, her hands were calloused from working with gymnasium equipment. On the occasions I saw her knees, I recognized the dark bruises of mat burns. It led me to wonder what her boyfriend must be like. Were American men all big? she asked me. I said that many were, since I knew it was what she wanted to hear. She also taught swimming, and her hair might be wet, her eyes bloodshot, when she met with me for a conversation.

Three times a week I met with Pius Michael Prutscher, a history major from Innsbruck. He was a handsome, apple-cheeked young man with full red lips and good white teeth. The teeth were unusual. In our second discussion he asked me what it was I did in Vienna for women. Pius greatly admired young men like myself, who had the strength of character to resist women, but when he found himself with a *Fräulein*—a word he pronounced like music—he could not help himself. It was as simple as that. Pius was also a very religious person, but when he saw a pretty *Fräulein* he forgot all about it.

When I saw Pius Prutscher, as I sometimes did, with one of these creatures he couldn't resist, I wondered what he would do if he saw the girls we had in California. Would he go nuts? It pleased me to be admired for my character, but there were times when I wondered about it. This good-looking American girl from Buffalo, taking courses at the university, proved to be so nearsighted that without her glasses she didn't recognize people until she spoke to them. Rather than be a girl who wore glasses, she was friendly with everybody. I liked her a lot, but I was never really sure, when she smiled at me, whom she was seeing. At meals I read the menu for her, and I kept her up to date about the news on the bulletin board. Once a month we had dances at the club I would take her to, then she would lose me. Anybody who cut in on her she would dance with, since we all looked alike.

Bogislav von Lindheim, the club secretary, had spent two years at Cambridge and spoke the English language the way I would have liked to. When we had dinner together all we spoke was English, since we had so much we wanted to discuss. He liked *Death in Venice,* by Thomas Mann, but his favorite writer was Kafka. I had never heard of Kafka. When I had learned enough German he would loan me some of his books.

Seen in profile, wearing his beret, Bogislav looked more like an eagle than a person. If Catherine had been able to *see* him, she would have been crazy about him. He had more women to talk to than he could find the time for, but he made extra time for me. When he had to go somewhere around Vienna I would tag along with him, and we would talk. Wherever he went he carried a leather valise that signified he was a scholar. He thought I should have one, so people would know who I was. I found that very strange coming from a person I considered so smart. We agreed on almost everything we discussed— with the exception of my liking Spengler—but it troubled me, when we were at the club, to see the way he would click his heels and bow when he met people. If it was a woman, he would lift her hand to his lips. There was quite a bit of that sort of thing at the club, but it was not one of the things we got around to discussing, like the way he never removed his rubbers. In time I figured out for myself that that was his way of saving the shoes he had bought in England.

Karl Fisher, from Dresden, worked most of the day, so I saw him only in the late afternoon. His father was an exporter of leather and fabrics, and Karl planned to go in the spring to Buenos Aires, where he would run a branch of his father's business. He spoke excellent Spanish as well as English, but he liked to talk with me just to keep in practice. Karl wore his hair even shorter than I did, clipped at the sides and rear so that his ears, like mine, stuck out. He was stocky, very energetic, and what I would have called back home a "go-getter." He also had plans to start a branch of the business in Mexico City, and if I would learn to speak Spanish he would like me to take it over. That's how he was. I could see he was shrewdly appraising me while we sat and talked. If we could find a place to sit in the alcove, at a window over-looking Schottengasse, we would have a *Butterbrot* and *Schokolade* while we talked and watched the people passing. Vienna was not like Paris. There were very few people walking the streets, and most of them were elderly, or idlers who were quick to cluster around a peddler. These men were not so frail as Hermann but they had similar rabbit-like faces and large sad eyes. It led me to recall what the German, Dr. Haffner, had said to Mr. Liszt on the freighter: "The situation in Germany is serious, but not hopeless; the situation in Austria is hopeless, but not serious."

The alcove windows of the club framed views of Schottengasse where it narrowed to enter the inner city. The sidewalk widened directly below us to make an area favored by peddlers and idlers, a sort of open stage. The peddlers wore bowlers, but most of the idlers were hatless, in dark topcoats that were too large for them. From the angle of our view at the window I could see their thin necks in their collarless shirts. Just like the unemployed back in the States, they were putting in the time, and welcomed the entertainment. One of these peddlers had a portable, collapsible table, on which he put out his wares. Two or three of the idlers, at a respectful distance, would watch him set himself up for business. There was no rush. Everything in good time. It almost seemed to come as a surprise to the peddler to note the interest he had attracted. He would greet the men before him with a tip of his hat, and they would nod. He would then hold up before them the pen he was selling, unscrew the cap, and display the point. One of the idlers would be encouraged to step forward and look at it closely. What he saw was always reassuring. Filling the pen with ink, wiping the point, making lines with the pen on a pad of paper, the pad, too, offered for examination, would require five or ten minutes and attract three or four more spectators. One of these spectators, more substantial-looking than the others, wearing a wool muffler and shiny rubbers, would ask to inspect the pen, and take the liberty of writing with it on the pad. What he saw so pleased him he would buy one. On second thought, as he counted out his money, he decided to buy another. Each came in a box. He would slip them into a pocket of his coat. One of the idlers, too, would buy one, writing out his name on the pad of paper, a pen of this sort surely being one of the things he most needed. Another would follow. Three, sometimes four or five pens would be sold.

I had watched this scene many times before I recognized the peddler's accomplice. He might sometimes wear a cap, and be burdened with parcels one of his companions would hold for him. He might begin as a scoffer, backing away until coaxed to come forward. He smiled and joked. He broke the ice. Jauntily he marched away, delighted with his purchase.

What was it about this drama that held me? The gestures were minimal and expressive. In the dusky winter light, under overcast skies, it was all black and white, like a movie. The scene arranged itself in a predictable manner. On my mind's eye it overlapped other scenes that I had casually collected, like snapshots. Charlie Chaplin or Buster Keaton would have performed it to perfection. Yet it did not cross my mind to take the picture I saw with a camera. I had bought a camera—not after seeing some pictures, but after talking about photographs with Karl. The few pictures I had taken might well have come with the camera. The picture I saw from the window, consisting of many exposures, overlapping images and complex emotions, was one I had captured on the mind's eye only, and separate from the one I saw in the street.

Not far from where I lived was the Dorotheum, a huge warehouse of a pawnshop run by the city. One day I went there with Bogislav, not knowing what I might see. In one of the first rooms we entered I saw this English Raleigh bike, with a four-speed Sturmey Archer gear. The bike was like new, the tires had inner tubes, there were tools, a pump, and a lamp with a generator that was turned by the front wheel. Having seen this marvel, I had to have it. On it I would see all that there was to be seen, high countries, low countries, beginning with Italy. Over and over I would save—I told myself—whatever it would cost me.

Until the day of the auction I was apprehensive that some greedy Austrian would beat me to it. Since I could not understand the rules and words of the bidding, Bogislav agreed to go along with me. Of the two dozen or more people who appeared, all but three or four of them bid on the Raleigh. One by one, as the price went up, they dropped out. I turned a deaf ear to what was happening. After what seemed forever, the bike was mine for 240 schillings. How much was that? About sixty-five dollars. More than I had planned to spend through the winter. Bogislav perceived what he had long suspected: Americans from the Far West were crazy.

Someone had swiped the valves from the inner tubes, so the tires were flat and couldn't be pumped up. I had to carry that bike, a heavy touring model, the four long blocks to Florianigasse, then up the four long flights of stairs to my room, where Hermann let me in. He, too, thought I would have a heart attack. Little did I care, knowing the treasure was mine. I had perspired so much I had to take off my clothes and wipe myself with a towel. In the dim glow of the lamp on my desk, I lay in bed and examined the bike. I was both wildly elated and depressed. It proved to be a single, inflated emotion. I was like Pius Prutscher, who was smart and knew better, but when faced with his lust he couldn't help himself. What would he think if he knew I had blown it on a bike, and not a woman?

Hermann proved a great support and consolation, since his admiration was even greater than mine. He had never before seen a Sturmey Archer gear, only in catalogues. He had never owned a bike but he knew a lot about them since he wrote the business letters for supplies to England. When the bike was placed upside down, with the wheels in the air, the pedals could be pumped and the gears operated. Everything worked. We were both out of our minds. I fell asleep reassured that my action had been mad, but like that of a foolhardy lover, fated. I could not help myself. Had it taken me more than twenty-three years to find that out?

When I complained to Hermann about the gray sunless days, he said I had come too late for the good October weather. From now on through the winter it would be gray and cold, with snow on the roofs and ice in the streets. It made him shudder to think about it. There were four rooms to Frau Unger's apartment, but two were closed off during the winter. Frau Unger and her daughter shared a bedroom, and Hermann slept on a cot in the kitchen. He liked that, being the one who shivered the most and caught the first cold. By the light of a lamp Frau Unger had shown me the furniture in the parlor, all of it covered with sheets, and protected from the sun by drapes at the windows. Her life had once been different. She unwrapped her big hands from a wad of apron to sing to me, with gestures, *"Wien und der Wein, Wien und der Wein!"* I had thought "flashing eyes" was a literary phrase until I saw hers.

We were leaning, Hermann and I, on the bedding

being aired at the window. Far off to the north, beyond the *schöne blaue Donau,* there were fleeting patches of sunlight. In the garden below the window an elderly couple, arm in arm, and stately, walked the gravel paths. I was struck by how erect and dignified they were. At the sharp right-angle turns at the corners, they pivoted in a military manner. I was amused by that, and continued to watch them as they made a full tour of the garden and returned to the door at the entrance. Just before reaching it they stopped, as if at a command. A moment passed, as if they were waiting for it to open, then the man extended his hand like a sleepwalker and approached the door. As his fingers touched it, they moved along the surface till he found the latch. The door opened inward, and they marched out.

I turned to Hermann, who said, "They can't see. It's a *blind Garten.*" He said *"blint,"* and I realized he had said it before, but I had not understood him. No one came to this garden but the blind, and that was why the paths were so symmetrical. So many steps to a turn, so many steps to a bench. The men carried canes, but they seldom used them. I had been reluctant to watch them from the window, since I thought they would think I was spying, but now that this seemed unlikely, I stood at the window whenever it was open. On one occasion I saw several couples marching as if to unheard music. I was witness to a parable, I realized, with many nuances and meanings, a visual metaphor that I found exciting. What I had seen from the window would prove—over the next fifty years—to be inexhaustible each time I looked.

On my way to the club I passed a public *Badehaus*. I surely needed a bath, but even more I needed to wash the clothes that I had been wearing for weeks. I discussed the problem with Hermann, and learned the cost of a bath was a matter of time. Each person had a booth, and paid for five, ten or fifteen minutes of hot water. My strategy was one I had practiced in college. I would wear my soiled clothes into the shower, work up a good lather, then rinse off, getting two baths for the price of one. There was nothing new about this practice in Vienna, except for the fact that it was strictly forbidden. But how would they ever know if I wrung out the clothes I had washed, then put them back on, wet, beneath my suit and raincoat. I would then sprint the quarter mile up Florianigasse to my room.

I did not share this strategy with Hermann before giving it a try. I paid for only ten minutes of hot water, not to arouse suspicion, and managed to wash my hair, two shirts, shorts and socks. The water was hot and plentiful, but it switched to cold while I was still rinsing. For years I had learned to do without a cold rinse. I pulled on my suit, stuffed the socks into my pocket, then sprinted up the grade in my unlaced shoes, already squishy with water. In my room I spread my wet clothes on the cold tile oven and got into bed. As I see it, the sprint up the grade had saved my life. It got me so warm I didn't feel a thing but the warmth of the bed and my pounding heart. I was not unaware that I had been a fool, and might easily come down with double pneumonia, but it seemed unimportant in the light of the challenge, the money I had saved and the strategic triumph. I lost a day at the club while my clothes were drying. Frau Unger transferred them to the warmth of her kitchen; she liked the wildness of my just washed hair and the high quality of my socks. I felt fine.

In the cloakroom at the club, and on the stairs up from the street, I sometimes observed the furtive exchange of secret signs and greetings among certain members. Hands were raised, as in "Heil Hitler," but the words that were exchanged escaped me. There was also a clasp of the hand that involved an intertwining of the fingers. It was none of my business, but I was curious, and eager to share such a secret handclasp.

I turned to my friend Pius Prutscher, an influential young man. He often gave speeches I did not understand in the courtyard of the university. His apple-cheeked face and ears flushed red with his emotions. He mocked those who asked foolish questions. It seemed to me he was marked for greatness. If he had a problem in resisting women, the women had a bigger problem in resisting him. It pleased me, at the club, to be one of those Pius always greeted and talked to. I often heard his voice at the back of the cloakroom, or hoarsely whispering in the washroom.

On a gloomy day that felt like snow, a chill wind blowing along the Ringstrasse, I came on a cluster of students huddled on the steps of the university. The doors were blocked by the police. At the club I learned that Pius Prutscher, among others, had been taken into custody.

Those who knew anything would not talk about it. On a walk with Bogislav (he wouldn't talk at the club), he told me that the Nazis were behind the trouble. Dollfuss was a decent person, but he was helpless, and the Heimwehr —the so-called home forces—were already Nazi forces. Pius and his friends were a secret organization with the purpose of overthrowing Dollfuss. What they wanted for Austria was a leader like Hitler. The slogan they exchanged in the dark of the stairs was *"Österreich über Alles, wenn wir nur wollen!"* (Austria over everything, if we only will it!)

On Kärntnerstrasse, even as we were talking, we passed a company of Austrian soldiers so nondescript and pathetic I thought they must be part of a movie. But no, they were the fatherland's soldiers. I thought this turn of events would bring us closer together, but Bogislav was so ashamed of what was happening I think he regretted telling me about it, like an illicit affair. He also felt that I was part of the new world, and that he was hopelessly part of the old one. Just seeing and talking to me made him feel worse, since I was always so damned upbeat and optimistic.

It was one thing for me to be low on money, since it was all part of my adventure, but Bogislav had only what he made teaching one course at the university. It shamed him to mention how little it was. I had also figured out that he was not from Salzburg, as he had told me. I had been to his closet-sized room. The only books he owned were in his valise. He sometimes read to me, as a joke, the advertisements for husbands in the *Neue Wiener Zei-*

tung, where *Fräuleins* might list a cow as part of their dowry, but he also hoped that he would find some fairy princess or countess, looking for a scholar and a poet.

He knew one countess, but she was Hungarian, and not his type. I had met her at the club, where she was playing Ping-Pong with another Hungarian. The Hungarians were great for Ping-Pong, and spent most of their time playing with each other. It was quite an occasion when they let me play. The way I served and held the paddle was so unusual it made a stir when I beat them. The Hungarian men, when they played with the countess, were smart enough to let her beat them, but when she played with me I didn't. She took the wooden paddle and broke it like a cookie, then stormed off. The Countess Maria Szapary was also a scholar, taking her doctorate in history at the university. She was a heavy, powerful young woman with frizzly orange hair, a broad flat face with small features. Her eyes were so wide apart I looked at just one at a time. They were sort of greenish, as in *"Ochy Chornia,"* but they sparkled like the eyes of Frau Unger, which seemed to be something special about Hungarians.

I thought I would never see the countess again, but she asked Bogislav if I would help her with her English. It was not appropriate for her to exchange conversations with a character who spoke the American language, so she would pay me four schillings an hour. That was fine with me, and we met at the club three or four times a week. The very idea of a countess seemed literary to me until I met Maria Szapary. Though she was built like a fullback, she was not unattractive. Every look she gave me was that of a woman looking at a man. In practical terms, of course, it didn't mean a thing since she was the Countess Szapary and a very Catholic Catholic. But it sure helped the time pass quickly when we talked. Her English was pretty good, for the usual sort of talk, but she was crazy to talk about religion. Did I believe in God? Why not? What was it, then, I *did* believe in? It wasn't just talk she wanted, but answers, and when she didn't get the answers she would actually curse me in Hungarian. I don't know why I liked that, but I did. I was also silenced by her emotion. I thought I could see her frizzly hair stand up from her scalp when she was in a rage. It didn't matter to her who might be listening. She was the Countess Szapary, from Abony near Pest, and everyone at the club kowtowed to her. Everybody but me. That often put her into one of her rages, but it also brought her back.

She loved American jazz, and we would drive around the city in a taxi looking for recordings of the Mills Brothers and Bing Crosby. At the dances I taught her how to Balboa. She took me to watch her play tennis at a club, where she served and volleyed like a cannon. She either double faulted or served an ace. For almost three weeks I did little else but talk with the countess, or sit and wonder about her, until she took off for a ski lodge in Switzerland. Bogislav told me she skied the way she did everything else.

We had our first snow, and my room was so cold I could see my breath like smoke in the morning. I bought a flannel bathrobe I could wear in my room or as the lining of my raincoat when I went to the club. The lint from the robe would come off on my coat sleeves, and I would have to stand in the dark of the cloakroom and pick it off. I would stay at the club until it closed, about ten, then take off on the double for my room, where I would get in bed with most of my clothes on until I warmed up.

Another problem I was having was with the *Butterbrot* and *Schokolade*. As hungry as I was, I found it hard to eat it. The thought of California orange juice drove me wild. I didn't look so good either, as my friend Karl Fisher told me; I had lost so much weight my clothes hung loose on me. There was a mirror high on the wall behind my washstand, where I could clearly see the room around me reflected, but not my own face. There was a face of sorts, more sallow than pale, the leaden whiteness like that of tallow, that I sometimes caught a glimpse of in shopwindows where I stood looking at something. I don't think I thought of it as my *self*. It couldn't be me, but I saw it in passing, and I still see it fifty years later, gray as the drizzle that concealed everything around me.

What I needed, Karl told me, was exercise. He rented a bike one Sunday, so we could ride out to the Wiener Wald together. There were many hikers in the woods, but few cyclists. The trees had lost their leaves, and I felt the melancholy of hikers and woods just before winter, both frail and vulnerable looking. If I looked sharp, I could often see lovers partially concealed in piles of leaves. Pius Prutscher had advised me it was not for him; he much preferred a bed.

43

Karl was amazed to see that I could pump up hills, weak as I was, that he would have to get off his bike and walk. I let him ride mine, and he wanted to buy it. He played a lot of soccer, and with his powerful legs he could pump up most grades without rising from the seat. We had our supper at an inn at the edge of the woods, where I drank quite a bit of what they called May wine, and joined in lustily with the singing of the *"schöne blaue Donau"* and other songs of that type. Karl said all I needed to make a good German was to eat more. The way I was feeling, it occurred to me that with winter coming, and the countess away skiing, I should take off for Greece or sunny Italy, but Karl had been to Italy, all the way to Naples and across the bay to the isle of Capri, and what impressed him more than anything else was how cold it had been in March! And here it was just December, with the coldest months still ahead.

Because I didn't look so good, and badly needed a change of diet, Karl suggested I go with him to visit a Frenchman who lived in a castle about a two-hour train ride up the Danube from Vienna. Monsieur Deleglise liked to meet young people, especially Americans. He had lived and traveled in the Far West, and the Hopi Indians had made him a chief. Karl thought I should meet such an unusual man. In the first war, he had fled from France to Canada to evade the draft. That cost him his French citizenship and he could not return after the war and live in France. He had first brought his family to Vienna, where his wife was a prima donna in the opera, but he had lost most of his money in the American stock market crash and moved his family to this castle in the Wachau. At Schloss Ranna, they lived pretty much as people did in the Middle Ages. It wasn't much for comfort, without heat or plumbing, but the food was unusually good and Karl doubted I would ever see anything like it. Schloss Ranna was there when Richard the Lion-Hearted came along the Danube on his way back to England after the Crusades. He may have stopped for the night. There was a crypt that dated from the eleventh century.

I would have liked an old castle at a warmer time of year, but I had recently seen the movie about a Connecticut Yankee in the court of King Arthur, and it led me to wonder what the Middle Ages were really like. The night before we took the train, we had our first real snow. In the morning my high window blazed with light from the white roofs, and snow concealed the gravel paths in the *blind Garten*. On my way to meet Karl I passed a plump beggar, barefoot in the snow, with a big shawl-wrapped woman holding a fat baby. The man stood with his palms pressed together, as if praying, with a slit at the top where coins might be inserted. The two of them sang carols in piercing, off-key voices. Frau Unger had warned me many times about well-fed beggars, who rented foundling babies and were all better fed than Hermann, but on more than one occasion I had observed her slipping coins between a beggar's pressed palms. She saw right through the performance, but whatever she saw, she thought it better to observe the custom. As I did. Watching the man shift from foot to bare foot in the snow, I could feel the chill at the roots of my teeth.

The train we took, a wood-burning locomotive with a big funnel stack, like the Burlington locals of my boyhood, had fresh-cut logs piled high on the tender instead of coal. It went along the north shore of the Danube, and on the wide curves I could see the cloud of smoke pouring from the stack. The one coach had three or four benches, like a streetcar, but there were only a few passengers. North and west of Vienna, where the valley opened, the river spread itself wide as a lake, with very little to show the current's direction. A flat-bottomed side-wheel river steamer, the paddles slapping the water, had the words BUDA-PEST painted on the fender, the hyphen between the words like the river between the two cities. In the great Mississippi flood of 1927 I had seen the river fan out wide around Cairo, and I wondered if the Marmon was still where we had left it in Lake Village, Arkansas, with my mouth organ under the front seat.

The local train made all the stops, and in the early afternoon it picked up kids on their way home from school. They either carried their books in a harness on their backs or had them bound up in long straps they could swing. They filled the coach seats, and two small boys sat on the wooden bench facing us. Both wore heavy hiking shoes with half socks, and lederhosen that exposed their pink scuffed knees. They were towheads, with almost white blond hair, and one had a shiny runner from his nose into his mouth. He had picked up right away, from the shoes I was wearing, that I was something foreign. His chubby legs were thrust toward me, showing

46

the bottoms of his shoes, his pudgy hands were pressed to the bench seat as if he feared to slip off. The cold and excitement had flushed his face so that it glowed like a ripe cherry. I couldn't seem to stare at him enough, and he felt the same about me. Karl Fisher saw such kids all the time, and once he had been one, but there was nothing at all like this boy in Vienna and I felt very close to him. Over the long Nebraska winters my nose, too, had drained into my mouth, both nostrils sore from the drag of my mitten, and the first snapshot of myself I had seen featured the same open-mouthed, adenoidal stare. This boy was spellbound until the train stopped, then he exploded like a spring-wind toy and tried to race off in all directions. From a high, snow-covered mound near the train he turned for one more long, incredulous look at me, shouted his defiance, then took off.

On the north side of the river I saw the ruins of castles, along with some not ruined, small villages huddled at their bases. The sun was shining in Krems, a town with a big station and a wide street full of cars and shoppers. There was a bridge across the Danube where it narrowed and Karl told me that Madame Deleglise, when the weather permitted, came to Krems for her baths. Once a year she might go to Innsbruck, or as far as Salzburg, for her shopping, but she no longer went to Vienna because she believed the Viennese gossiped about her, which of course they did. The gossip was that her husband, Monsieur Deleglise, kept her captive in one of the rooms at Schloss Ranna. The facts were that he didn't have to keep her captive, since there was simply no money for her to travel, or escape. Once they had traveled all over, to India, China and the Yucatán, from where Madame Deleglise had all but died on the long sea voyage to Europe.

Karl never actually said so, but the impression I got was that Monsieur Deleglise was something of an oddball, and that appealed to me. He had tried being a native in the South Seas, and being an Indian in Arizona, and since the stock market crash he had tried living in the Middle Ages.

Out the window I could see that the river had narrowed and we had left the spread of the valley behind us. When I looked back, the view was like a postcard, with the river dark between banks of snow, the sun still gleaming on the ruins of the castles. Up ahead we were entering a gorge, with the river in deep shadow. The last of the kids had left the train at Krems and we had the coach to ourselves. I sat at one window, and Karl had moved so he could sit at another. He was usually fidgety, slapping his knees and clasping his hands, but he sat there in a brown study. The sudden change from Krems, where the sun had been shining, the streets gleaming where the snow had melted, was like that of crossing an invisible boundary or rising to where the air seemed thinner and colder. A cold draft of air entered the coach when the conductor looked in on us, a ruddy-faced old man with a walrus moustache, the dangling ends stained with tobacco. When he spoke to us without removing his pipe, I saw a washer attached to the stem, green as the bit in the mouth of a horse. With it, although his teeth were parted, the pipe stayed in his mouth while he mumbled.

We left the train in Spitz, the river black in the gorge below us, the city dark and silent behind. Only one car had left its tracks in the road we followed to the west. Where this road dipped to the left, to follow the bend in the river, another road forked to the right up a narrow canyon. Nothing at all had come down this road since it had snowed. On the river below us, veiled by smoke from its stack, a steamer drifted in the current, its side-wheels slapping the water, with people out on the deck who waved to us. I waved in return. All my life, from wagons, from cars and trains, from windows and elevations, or across empty spaces, from anything that seemed to be moving, I had waved at people, and they had waved at me, but only here did it occur to me how remarkable it was.

In that cold air, veiled with the smoke of our breathing, I seemed to see Richard the Lion-Hearted, on whom I had once written a term paper, cold and clammy in his suit of clanking armor, only his black eyes glinting at the visor of his helmet, weary in mind and aching in body, eaten alive by lice and gnawed with fear and suspicion, uncertain of friend and foe and whether he would ever get back to his homeland, with a large pack of vassals and hangers-on to account for, along with numerous baying dogs, thieves and beggars, pause for a moment right where we were standing, to peer down at a black, alien river he would never see again—not a great figure in history, carrying a shield, but a flesh-and-blood bully

49

who was saddle sore and homesick. Far to the east, where the sun was still shining, the landscape was like a painting on glass through which I could see back to where I had come from, where great rivers like this one, just for starters, did not flow from the south to the north, but from the north to the south. How Richard the Lion-Hearted had felt was not strange to me.

We had an hour's walk to Muhldorf, Karl told me, then another short hike to Schloss Ranna. The brightness of the winter sky lit up the floor of the canyon, but the trees, shrubs and walls fencing us in were black. Under the snow to the left of the road I could hear water running. The air had the tang of wood smoke. Here and there on the upper slopes I could see the black stitching of grapevines.

Where the snow had blown thin on the road, a sledge had come to a stop. It was hard for me to tell which way it was headed since it was made of two saplings, on which the logs were piled, then drawn up like a bow to form a hammock. At what proved to be the rear, an old man crouched on one of the logs, smoking his pipe. "Greet God!" he said to us, and we said to him, "Greet God!"

I hadn't heard that greeting before, and I liked it. Stretched out behind him was a long branch that he used as a rudder. Was he waiting for it to snow again? What was I to think? From farther up the trail I glanced back to see him, the light glinting on the nickel cap to his pipe.

I had to stop several times to tap the caked snow out of my shoes. I was no longer cold, the climb had warmed me, but the shiny film on my eyes made everything I

50

looked at glitter like tinsel. We were both too winded to
talk, and would just stand together, wheezing like sprint-
ers. Somewhere up ahead of us a door closed with a
bang. A plume of white smoke, so close we could taste
it, had drifted down the canyon from a village, and as we
approached it I could see that the mill wheel was frozen
in the ice. Strewn around the pond were loose barrel
staves left by kids who had cleared away the snow from
a small piece of the ice. We could see the scratches made
by their skates. Four or five cabins, plus an inn, were set
at the narrowest point in the canyon, like a cork. A small
bulb burned at the porch of the inn, where a man, with
his knees cocked, arched a stream of urine over the porch
rail into the mound of snow behind it. He moved the
stream slowly from side to side, as if watering a lawn. I
was amazed at how such a small man managed to pee so
long.

"Greet God!" Karl greeted him, and he did the same.
Another man's suit coat, a lot too big for him, hung to
below his knees. Around his pants legs, like leggings, he
had wrapped strips of burlap. As he buttoned up—he
seemed to be in no hurry—he asked Karl where it was we
were from. "Vienna," Karl replied. The man stared at us
in silence, but in his white face I could see the dark hole
formed by his lips.

Between two of the cabins the snow had melted on a
mound of straw and manure. On the slope behind it, far
back where the last of the sun's rays warmed it, a bell
tower rose from a clump of buildings with conical roofs
and tiny windows. In one window a light burned, like a

star. Far away though it seemed, I could hear hounds baying, or just one hound repeated by echoes.

What might have been a narrow road led up from Muhldorf to pass an onion-domed church, in a cluster of trees and buildings, but Karl followed a trail that went to the north along the rim of the canyon. Everything below us was in shadow, as if we saw it in clear deep water. The houses were scattered about along the canyon bottom, and I could see a dark figure walking a lantern. The sounds of water rising in the neck of a pump, then spilling into a pail, grew louder as they rose toward us. Just to the north of the village another pond spread wide, the ice blue as skimmed milk where the kids had cleaned it. Two small boys played silently with a sled. One of them glanced upward and saw us, and I thought he would wave or holler but he didn't.

Another trail, concealed by the new snow but visible in the slanting light, crossed a field of stubble on the slope to the square blockhouse at one side of an orchard. As we stood there wheezing, catching our breath, an ear-splitting clamor sounded directly above us, the echoes rolling and colliding around us.

"Good," Karl said, calmly. "The bell is for *Jause.*"

He had told me about *Jause,* an Austrian custom of getting in more food between dinner and supper, but if what I had heard was a bell, I felt the ringer must be crazy. I stood with my head down, my shoulders hunched up, in case it came again. The thought of food, however, spurred us both on and we were soon across the slope to the level of the orchard. A path had been trampled between the trees to a cluster of outbuildings in a sort of hollow. Right where we were standing, in the shadow of the blockhouse, a low rock wall ran along one side of the path that led to the entrance. I thought I saw shrubs growing behind it. I took a seat on the wall, to empty the snow from my shoes, then turned to peer into a huge trench, deep and wide, in which full-grown trees were rooted. The tops of these trees I had mistaken for bushes. I was on the rim of a dry moat, at the entrance to the Middle Ages. The walls of the moat were dark, but the snow at the bottom was as wide as, or wider than, a two-lane highway. I was so flabbergasted I said nothing. The vast bulk of the castle, visible through the archway, was like that of an ocean steamer docked at a pier, the deck looming high above us. The upper part of the wall was whitewashed, luminous in the reflected snow light, but at eye level the plaster had peeled away to expose the rock foundation. The moat circling Ranna had been created by building the bulk of the structure on its own rock island.

A singsong coaxing voice, like a farmer's calling pigs, could be heard, and I saw the movement of shadows cast by a lantern. Karl stood at the low wall of the ramp, beckoning to me. In the deep shadows below us, where the snow was trampled, I could see what I thought was a pack of dogs following a man who swung a lantern. The enclosure below us was large as a farmyard, and curved away into the darkness behind the castle. As the man passed directly below us, swinging the lantern, the shadows cast on the wall of the castle had antlers. Karl called to him and he stopped and hoisted his light toward us. I could see he was hatless. His breath plumed like smoke from his mouth. In a low voice, not unlike gargling, as if he spoke with a mouthful of marbles, he said something to Karl. "And how is the Meister?" Karl asked him, but I did not understand his answer. As we turned away, I said, "Who is the Meister?"

"Monsieur Deleglise," said Karl. "They all call him the Meister."

We followed the narrowing ramp to the entrance, the huge door ajar, into a dim corridor worn to a gutter at the center. At the corridor's end I could see the sky like a piece of stained glass. On our left we entered a court, open to the sky. Stairs along the back wall mounted to a balcony landing. With a broom on the landing, Karl swept off our shoes before we entered a dark, stone-floored hallway, the floor sprinkled with snow from a slotted open window on the stairs. In the archway on our left, a wide door, with a latch. Karl rapped sharply on the door before we entered.

The room was long, with a low timbered ceiling, and a heavy table with a dozen or so high-backed chairs stood at its center. At the far end of the table a small bulb glowed in the hub of a wagon-wheel chandelier. The window in the alcove at the end of the room glowed with the winter sunset. Just in front of the alcove, a big glass tank filled with murky green water filtered the light.

To the right of the door we had entered, logs were piled along the wall behind a stove that was metal, not tile, and gave off heat. The sides were warm, rather than hot, so that I could stand with my backside to it, soaking up the warmth. I had got so cold on the long walk up from the river that the sudden warmth gave me the shivers, the way it used to in Omaha when, after hours of sledding or skating, I would stand on one of the floor radiators and bask in the smell of my clothes drying. How far away all of that seemed, but the smell had not changed.

Karl took a slice of bread from the basket on the table, spread it thick with butter, and shared it with me. Back in Vienna I would have said no, *danke,* but I gulped it down. When the door quietly opened at my back, the person who entered thumped into me. It startled him so much to find somebody there, he threw up his hands, knocking his hat from his head, and almost teetered over backward until Karl grabbed him. He picked up the hat he had dropped on the floor and stood honing the brim on his coat sleeve. I had never seen an uglier man. His head was loaf-shaped—he gave me time to look it over —with a crease at its center in which a few black hairs were like wires connecting his ears. His color was dark brown, like saddle leather, but there was nothing in his face to indicate his forehead or his eyebrows. Nor any chin at all, that I could determine, so that he looked like a fish seen from the front in an aquarium.

Karl took a lot of time to tell him who I was, and where I was from. At the mention of the word "America," he looked dazed. Karl was saying that Uncle James, which was what he was called, had been with Monsieur Deleglise in the United States, where, among other things, he had managed Madame Deleglise's career as an opera singer. To all this Uncle James was silent, as if his memory had failed him. Against the fading light in the alcove I could see a single long-tailed goldfish suspended as if anchored in the tank of murky water. A small, stooped figure in a fur hat pointed like a dunce cap—I first thought it might be an old woman in a turban—stood dropping into the tank small pellets of food, which fell to where the goldfish gulped them like bait. The white body of the fish was so transparent the fat sack of the belly was visible, stuffed with the pellets like a bag of shot.

Having turned to see what it was I was looking at, Karl called out a greeting, then led me back to meet Monsieur Deleglise. He gave me his small cold hand, and in a voice pitched so high it might have been a child's, he repeated phrases of greeting in English, French and German. A gray stubble concealed his face, and the soggy butt of a cigarette, stuck to his lower lip, bobbed as he talked. Karl explained to me that the fur hat he was wearing had been given to him by the Hopis when they made him a chief. We came back to the table, under the chandelier, where Monsieur Deleglise placed the fur hat on the seat of his chair like a cushion, then sat on it. Doing this seemed to please him, but the smile he gave me was hard to tell from a grimace.

Karl took the place on his left, Uncle James on his right, and I took the seat to the left of Karl. A blond young man with short hair, a crisp toothbrush mustache and pale water-blue eyes sat across from me. His name was Beps. Karl explained again what a scholar I was, how much I had traveled, and how in the spring I would go to Italy, and then to Paris. Monsieur Deleglise was skeptical of Americans, but impressed. We ate bowls of potato soup served by a hefty young woman with suds drying on her plump white arms. Uncle James called her Mizi. As she leaned over me to serve the soup, I noticed her black almond eyes in a creamy white face; her breath smelled of warm milk.

We also had a fruit compote, the apples small as walnuts, then a demitasse of thick black coffee. How did I like it? I said I loved it. Uncle James advised me it was half chicory. Good coffee and tobacco were very dear in Austria. I was not asked, but later I talked about Chicago, about California, and the wonderful life I had led and was living. We all smoked a full pack of my Old Gold cigarettes and two of the smaller packets of Falk Bubies, the brand favored by Monsieur Deleglise. I liked their mildness, but they were very dry and flared up like excelsior when I lit them.

I learned from Uncle James that the suit and pants he wore, likewise the Stetson hat, were purchased in Cedar Rapids, Iowa, the scene of Madame Deleglise's greatest triumph, in *La Fanciulla del West*. I observed that Uncle James, whenever we all got to laughing, popped sugar cubes into his mouth before he took a sip of his coffee. Monsieur Deleglise ate very little, but he enjoyed the talk. He plucked the soft centers from slices of bread and rolled them into pellets the size of BBs, which he left on his plate. After the coffee we had glasses of hard cider, the same murky green color as the water in the fish tank. Without much prodding I told them about Death's Corner in Chicago, Larrabee and Blackhawk, where I had seen men shot at and found one who had been killed, with the holes across his back like a row of buttons. That got me a pop-eyed stare from Uncle James, but I could see that Beps didn't believe a word of it. At one point a husky fellow, the sleeves rolled up on his hairy arms, his shoulders so wide his head looked small, came in with a big tray and gathered up the dishes like the world's happiest busboy. He did it fast, but took the trouble to leave the pellets Monsieur Deleglise had rolled on his napkin, where they looked like rabbit turds.

When the time came for me to get up from the table, I preferred to just sit there. The shoes I had left to dry out beneath the stove would not go back onto my feet. I went along in my socks, carrying my shoes, Monsieur Deleglise leading with a candle up the wide stone stairs in the hall and into a long low room, like the one we had just left, the eyes glinting in the antlered trophies on the walls and all the furniture covered with sheets. In the adjoining room we could see our breath smoke, but I couldn't breathe. The stench was so intense it was like something other than air. Monsieur Deleglise walked with his candle to open wide one of the high casement windows. "Frish air!" he cried. "Frish! Frish! Frish!" If he liked a word he loved to repeat it. The room was like a loft with a high ceiling, empty of everything but two folding army cots. One was covered with a dark, coarse-haired pelt. "Moose! Moose! Moose!" Monsieur Deleglise chanted, and he shuffled about with his candle, like a dancing Indian. "He shot it in Canada," Karl explained, and Monsieur Deleglise shouted, "Bang! Bang! Bang!" I could see how the Hopis must have loved him. He wished us a *Gute Nacht,* a *Schlafen Sie wohl,* then he went off with the candle and left us standing there in the dark. But I could see the white walls, in the reflected roof light, and on the wall that I faced, fire shadows were playing. They came through the window of a room across the open court.

"Whose room is that?" I asked.

"Madame Deleglise." We reflected on that in silence. "She sleeps most of the day," he added, "but she likes to read at night."

"What's she read?" I asked him.

He replied, "French novels."

I don't know why it pleased me so much to hear that. A woman who was captive, in a castle like this, who spent her nights reading French novels. I warmed up after a while, lying under the moose hide, and noticed that the snowflakes blowing in the window were prickling my face. After the day I had had, it seemed natural to me that the old man with the sledge of logs below Muhldorf was finally going to get the snowfall he needed. I didn't need it, but I liked its cool prickle on my hot face.

Four

etween sleeping and waking, I seemed to hear the faraway sound of ore boats honking on Lake Michigan. I was troubled when this honking faded, followed by a muffled thump. I opened my eyes on a blaze of sunlight, a cloud of sparkling snow at the open window. A hood of this snow, like a lacy nightcap, had settled on my hair. As the air at the window cleared, I could see a big fellow straddling the peaked roof across the court, a cowlick of straw-colored hair concealing his forehead, his cheeks flaming as if with a fever, his eyes popped wide, his mouth open, as if he had just shouted Hallelujah!

I had read about the legendary Till Eulenspiegel, and I thought at last I had seen him. Two or three flannel shirts, one worn over the other, opened at the collar, gave him the look of a crazy plant in flower. As I stared at him he cupped his mittened hands to his mouth and made the mournful sound of a steamboat honking. It seemed the longest time before I heard—as if it came from the river—the rolling echo. Across his lap he held a pole, with a scraper at one end, which he dipped into the blanket of roof snow, then leaned his full weight on it as if he was poling a boat. The wide swath of snow fell with a thundering *bomp* into the court. The puffing cloud of snow dust soon concealed him, but behind it I could hear him making the *bomp* sound. Really crazy. In his shoes, I might have done the same thing myself.

My friend Karl's bed was empty, the bedding turned back to air. I tapped the snow out of my shoes, managed to get them on my feet, then went out through the door we had entered, across the room with the sheet-covered furniture, and down the stairs to the floor below. Snow had blown in through the slotted window, powdering the stairs. I first knocked on the door, as Karl had done, then peered into the room, to find it empty, but several places were set at the far end of the table. No food had been left on three of the plates, but Monsieur Deleglise had plucked the soft centers from several slices of bread and rolled them into pellets. They were all on his plate, with the soggy butts of several cigarettes.

I buttered the slice of bread I found in the basket and walked to stand at the alcove window. Fresh snow had covered the millpond in the canyon. A man standing on

61

the porch of the inn slapped his bare hands together, as if applauding.

There proved to be two fish in the fish tank, one like an egg that had just been dropped into boiling water, with the white oozing out. The fins of both fish were like transparent veils, but their undulating movement did not move them. The one with the shot-like pellets in his belly was like an anchored balloon.

On my legs and feet, as if a door stood open, I could feel a cold draft. It came from beneath a wide door in the left wall. I thought it must be a hallway, and peered behind it: a gloomy darkness, smelly and chill as a basement, but nothing I could see. The first match I struck blew out in the draft. I lit another, cupped it in my hands, then glanced up to see the staring eyes and gleaming teeth of a black savage. Over his head, ready to strike, he held a tomahawk. Lucky for me, the match I held flickered and went out. In the semidarkness, my heart pounding, I could make out the figure of a cigar store Indian on a pedestal. Along with his protuberant staring glass eyes, he had a partial set of human teeth. That's where I was when Karl, red-faced with cold, rushed in from the main hallway to yell at me. Had I eaten? What a fine day it was! There would be time for me to look at the Indian relics later, but right now, on such a day there was no time to lose! The Meister was ready and waiting for us in the orchard.

I followed Karl out to the landing, down the stairs, into the court, already half filled with snow pushed from the roofs. As we crossed the court Karl glanced at the sky as if he thought a piece of it might fall on him. In the dark corridor that led out to the ramp, Joseph rumbled past us pushing a wheelbarrow piled with snow. He wore a cane-sided chauffeur's cap and military breeches, but I recognized him as the smiling fellow so eager to clear away the dishes from the table. Out on the ramp, in the blinding snow glare, Karl told me that all of the snow that fell *inside* Schloss Ranna had to be shoveled up and carted out before it melted and turned to ice. There were rooms beneath the courts, and then rooms beneath them, along with a secret corridor, it was rumored, that led from Ranna to what had been a monastery in Unter Ranna. The thought of it made him excited. Snow was already melting at the edge of the pitched roofs, exposing shingles that were black as wet coal. Below us, to the south, the stubbled field sloped away to the cluster of white roofs in Muhldorf. Beyond the village, far across the valley, blue wooded ridge after ridge receded to the shimmering horizon. A zigzagging row of poles, supporting a wire like a clothesline, came up from Muhldorf to the rim of the orchard, then came up through the trees to enter the archway. From there it stretched across the moat like a sagging aerial, to a small slotted window in the white wall. Everywhere the sun shone, water was dripping. Karl scooped up a handful of the moist snow, pressed it into a ball, threw it into the blue canyon that spread behind us. A moment later we heard it fall with a plop.

Where that snowball had landed, Karl pointed out to me, there had once been a monastery. We could see the clearing, with a wall around it, that had been the garden. Kids playing on the slope across the creek had heard the snowball plop and peered up at us. Several dogs barked. I had the fleeting impression of being so high above it all that there was no connection between upper and lower Ranna, except for those who were below and looked up at it. They did not call out, or wave, or shake tiny fists at us. Their small white faces had no features. Was this how one should look if seen from heaven? It crossed my mind.

Karl had taken me by the arm to turn me around. He pointed through the archway into the orchard, where a big black-splotched creature, the size of a calf, gamboled about between the trees. He dipped his head, like a scoop, to toss up gobs of snow, which he then tried to catch, snapping his huge jaws. A small piping voice called to him. I heard clapping hands. The huge dog wanted to frisk about, like a puppy, but the footing was uncertain. Once he fell, like a structure collapsing. Monsieur Deleglise, who looked dwarfed beside him, clapped his hands above his head like a flamenco dancer. This was a game they both liked and were eager to play. The great dog reared up, a full head taller than the man, to place his paws on the man's narrow shoulders, his tongue licking his face. That knocked off his fur hat and the two of them stood there, as if grappling, the dog's long tongue stroking his face and hair until the man toppled over backward, straddled by the dog. Like two kids playing in the snow, one of them a lot bigger than the other, Deleglise lay out on his back, while the dog licked his face like a plate of gravy. He just lay there, grinning like a gargoyle, until Karl pulled the dog off him and I hoisted him to his feet. There seemed to be little to him but the clothes he was wearing, the brown mackinaw over an old army sweater. When I gave him his hat he pulled it down so that it covered his face. Why hadn't Karl told me he was crazy? With his face concealed, he looked headless.

"We walk! We walk!" he piped. "Yes?"

"Ja-jah!" Karl replied. "We walk!"

When Deleglise spoke to the dog, he went off at a loping canter, leading the way. The trail we followed led to a deep ravine full of shrubs and trees, with a creek at its bottom. As we stood there we could hear the water purling beneath the snow. At a clearing on the steep slope Deleglise crouched like a child, his legs thrust out before him, and slid on the seat of his pants to the bottom. This got the dog so excited he ran up and down the rim, baying hoarsely, until he found another way into the ravine. In the silence that followed his rumbling bark we could hear doors slamming, and the voices of women.

I refused to sit and slide in my only pair of pants, so I walked to where I could climb down, hanging on to shrubs and bushes. The village was just ahead of us, in a small clearing, with the houses set into the foot of the ridge below Ranna. Not a soul was in sight as we walked in, the dog gamboling ahead of us.

"Where's everybody?" I asked.

"It's Prince," said Karl. "They don't believe he's just a dog."

At one of the dark cabin windows I saw a face, like a goblin's, with a child's big staring eyes and a wild thatch of hair. Someone yanked him away. In the fresh fall of snow around the porch of the inn, several customers had already relieved themselves. Deleglise had shuffled ahead to a house on the left, where he paused to rap his knuckles on the door. In the silence this seemed a great racket. A dog whimpered in one of the nearby cabins. A young woman opened the door, a shawl about her shoulders, her hands rolled up in a wad of her apron. She greeted Deleglise as the Meister. For a moment their high-pitched voices were like those of two gossiping women. The Meister turned to beckon to us. "Come, come, come!" he piped, and we followed him into a dark room that seemed barren. One chair sat beside a rocking cradle. A young man had risen just as we entered, to stand beside the young woman. I thought her plump figure and round face attractive. He was much more nervous than she was. The Meister introduced me as the scholar from America. They admired me, my clothes, my shoes, and marveled that I could speak their language. The Meister stooped to look at the child, in the shadow of the crib hood, commented on its plumpness, its health, its dark hair, then took several coins from his pocket and dropped them on the crib comforter. In response to their thanks, bowing, their hands clasped, I understood him to mention that Ranna needed wood, as one might mention in passing that an ogre needed food. The huge dog stood waiting for us at the door. No one appeared in the street as we walked away and followed the stream bed up the canyon. The dog led the way.

"What a handsome couple," I said to Karl.

The Meister muttered something I did not understand.

"He wants you to know," said Karl, "that it is not his child."

I said, "How come?"

"Out here," Karl replied, "the war took all of the young men. There are many young women who will never have husbands but who are capable of having babies. If she has a healthy baby she attracts the young men. The baby, not the father, is what is important. When they saw her healthy male baby she had many proposals, some of them from as far as Spitz."

"That's hard to believe," I said, eager to believe it, and wondered who the lucky father was. Were more volunteers needed? We were walking up an incline that made it difficult to talk. My shoes slipped badly in the powdery snow. During the morning the kids had been at play on the millpond I could see from the alcove window. A road went along the east side of the canyon, rising toward open country, with fewer trees. The dog had gone ahead of us to a point on the trail to which he seemed accustomed, and sprawled waiting for us. In the large black splotch on his face his small eyes were not visible, and

I missed them. How was one to guess what such a huge creature was thinking?

We all huddled together for a moment to catch our breath. Deleglise breathed hoarsely through his open mouth, a soggy butt attached to his lower lip. As he talked, it bobbled. He seemed indifferent to its being there. We stood wheezing, our breath veiling our faces, and I happened to glance back down the canyon at Schloss Ranna, the windows blazing like fire. The whole inner bulk of Ranna seemed to float on the crest of a frothy wave. Not particularly high, not in the usual cloud-land of fairy castles, but at a remove that a small boy, looking upward, could appreciate. A remove with a connection. An actual Meister who occasionally made house calls, with a monster that was neither a hippogriff nor a dog, but something in between.

"It's out of this world!" I said.

"Out of! Out of!" the Meister echoed. In the deep shadows at Ranna's base the village appeared to be under water. Ribbons of wood smoke curled to fray on the sky. "Yes, yes," he repeated. "It is out of!" What I had said seemed to reassure him. He gazed at me soberly, the soggy butt at his lips wagging, the cold air filming his gray eyes. "You like—yes?"

"I've never seen anything like it," I replied.

He turned from me to speak to Karl, his head wagging. The fur hat tilted forward to conceal his eyes.

"He wants to know," Karl asked me, "if you would like to extend your visit. You are welcome to stay for a week if you would care to."

I turned to look at the Meister, his mother-of-pearl teeth set in a grin-like grimace, or a grimace-like grin. He looked cold, and frail as a medieval beggar.

"You stay, you stay—yes?"

I was eager to stay, but I was also convinced that Monsieur Deleglise, the Meister, was mad as a hatter. "Yes, yes!" I said.

From the chest pocket of his jacket he took a packet of cigarettes, offered me one, took one himself. Karl was not a smoker. He watched us light up and blow smoke at each other. Back down the trail we had come up, at the edge of the millpond, I could see several dogs waiting and watching; just behind the dogs, a cluster of furtive children. When we made a move toward them, both dogs and children scattered. The trail followed the creek bed back through the village, passing beneath the encircling outer walls of Ranna, then cutting through the ruins of the monastery. The dog galloped ahead of us to where the trail forked to the left, rising steeply up the bank to the slope below Ranna. From the rim of the canyon he peered down at us like a gargoyle. Above and behind him, the clatter of the bell seemed to come from the sky. In the clear dazzle of light it seemed louder, and more manic, than when I had heard it the previous evening, an ear-splitting, shrieking clamor. The air appeared to vibrate with it. The dog bayed.

"What madman is that?" I asked Karl.

"Antone," he replied, "the bell ringer."

On my mind's eye I could see him straddling the roof

peak, his red cheeks blazing, red-mittened hands cupped to his mouth.

"He's a big fellow?" I asked. "Yellow hair, red mittens?" I could see his thick hams tight in his overalls, straddling the roof.

"You've met him?"

"I've seen him."

Karl gave me a sly smile, said, "He's very popular with the ladies."

"I can believe that," I replied.

"He makes babies. He's the baby-maker."

"That makes him the real father of his country," I said, but that was lost on Karl, who said, "I'm famished!" and led off up the trail. As frail and weak as the Meister looked, he had the wind and endurance of a climber. Tortoise-like, if we passed him he came shuffling along and went by us. Crossing the slope beneath Ranna, I could hear myself wheezing. By the time we reached the landing at the top of the stairs my ears buzzed like magnetos. The Meister swept us all off, with a broom, then removed his own three-buckle galoshes, and I saw that all he was wearing was wool socks pulled over the feet of his flannel pajamas, like those I had worn as a child. He looked like a child, as he stood before us, his dunce hat tilted back on his head, a child whom a loving and indulgent father had draped with his own coat to keep from freezing. "Eat! Eat!" he piped, his eyes creased in a grin, and walked ahead of us into the warm dining *Saal,* where an aging bulldog, with clouded eyes, wearing a soiled and slobbered-on turtleneck sweater, lay curled up but shivering in a wicker basket beside the stove.

"Madame has come to dinner," Karl said to me, and there she was.

Back under the chandelier, a strong nasal declared, "Who is Merkun? Is from See-tar Rabids?" She sat at the table, her large protuberant eyes shining with expectation. Whatever they had told her, I knew she was doomed to disappointment. Her dark, lined face resembled that of the dog in the wicker basket. She was seated on a pillow, to get the proper elevation, her small broad hands like those of a farm child. Uncle James had risen, his napkin dangling from his collar, to make a formal and lengthy introduction. Several times he repeated the word *diva*. I understood little else. She gave me one of her hands, the plump, stubby fingers cluttered with rings. Her sad eyes searched my face for what she knew to be missing. Only a child had looked at me so boldly. At the part in her glossy black hair, the roots were whiter than her scalp.

As if none of this fuss concerned him, the Meister sat at his place, reading a newspaper. Uncle James proposed a toast, then made a toast, repeating the names of the cities where she had triumphed: "Venice, Palermo, Buenos Aires, Mexico City, Vancouver and See-tar Rabids!"

"Hear! Hear!" Karl cried, raising his glass of cider. Madame Deleglise was not flustered by this praise. It was part of her continuing performance. The glimpses I had of her profile reminded me of Mussolini. Her voice, like his, was big, but fuzzy with hoarseness, as if she had a bad cold. In the large bowl of soup she had been served was the skull of a dog-like head, the sharp teeth still set in the jaws. To get at bits of meat around the teeth and eye sockets she used a metal nut pick. Her spirits were high. She laughed "Ho-ho-*ho!*" like one of the seven dwarfs.

Uncle James wore a dinner jacket, with tails, a black bow tie on his yellow wing collar. Sugar syrup glistened on his lips. His role was that of host, a master of ceremony. When had I last been in See-tar Rabids? He was careful to mimic her pronunciation. Madame spoke little English, but she understood it, and laughed hoarsely at my comments. At these moments I noticed the glances she gave her husband. Animal. One that turns from its food to growl at a rival. I could imagine her shrieking, her black eyes flashing, before the gawking, upturned faces of See-tar Rabids. To light her cigarette Uncle James swept the napkin that dangled from his neck over the table. She exhaled slowly, enjoying its fragrance.

"Tell him," she said to Karl, "I have sons in Switzerland. One is big and stronk as he is."

Karl told me.

"Will they be home for Christmas?" I asked her.

"How would I know!" she bellowed. "He tells me nothing!"

"They write to you," he replied, calmly. "They do not write to me."

"They tell me nothing! They write I want, I want, I want!"

"Jacques wants skis," the Meister replied, matter-of-factly.

72

"To keel himself? Bah! Marcel wants fur gloves, for skating, a Cossack hat of chinchilla."

The Meister turned back to his paper. When speaking to his wife he showed no anger, but his face seemed to be cast in a different mold, no crazy wrinkles of mirth around his eyes.

Sensing that Madame was about to leave, Uncle James rose quickly and hurried to stand at the back of her chair. As she slid from the cushion he drew the chair aside, and there she stood, hardly higher than when she had been seated. Had she been seen as a precocious child? A miniature prima donna? She had put aside scraps of food for the dog, which she carried back to the door with her. The dog whimpered and slobbered, hearing her approach. "Dolly! Dolly!" she cried, stooping to feed her the scraps. We could hear the clop-clop of the loose jowls. For a moment Madame stood with her backside to the stove, her short legs concealed by a pair of galoshes, worn to keep her feet warm while she was dining.

"*Une grande plaisir a faire votre connaissance,*" she called to me, at which point I arose and bowed. To Karl she said, "*Ciao!*"

"*Ciao,*" he replied.

Uncle James opened the door, then turned to pick up the basket with the old dog. He followed her out in the hall, drew the door closed, and we heard their voices as they went up the stairs.

The Meister said, "He is an artist. He is an actor. Molière could not have done better."

Very simply, Karl said, "He loves her."

"I also," replied the Meister, "but I am no actor."

Karl avoided the glance I gave him, said, "I've got to pack my bag. It's a long walk to Spitz." He got up to leave, then turned and said, "You're sure you're staying?"

I was no longer so sure. I envied him his leaving. I thought of my life in Vienna with pleasure. To sleep in a real bed seemed dreamy. But neither did I want to hurt the Meister's feelings. His shadowed face, with the light on his wispy white hair, was like that of a child. Did I like him? Or did I just feel sorry for him?

"Go! Go!" he cried, shrilly. "Go if you like!"

Which was why I stayed. It's as simple as that.

"I'm staying," I said to Karl. "I'll see you soon."

"Sure," Karl said. "Anything I can send you?"

"I've got a card you can mail," I replied, as an excuse to leave the room with him. As we mounted the stairs to the second floor we could see the fire reflections behind Madame's door, and hear the wood crackle. Uncle James was laughing and talking.

"He *is* an actor," Karl said. "When she comes to dinner he gives a performance."

Although the window to our room stood open, the stench was still in the air, like that of wet paint. "I'll leave you this," Karl said, handing me his tube of toothpaste. "If you want to shave, ask Mizi for hot water."

"What's this *Meister* stuff about?" I asked.

He seemed reluctant to tell me. "Why bother?" he said. "For you he's Monsieur Deleglise."

"It's not a bother," I said. "I think I sort of like it."

74

"That's what they call him. That's the way they feel about him. Unter Ranna, Ober Ranna—it's all of a piece, or pieces." He waved his arms at the window. "Whoever lives at Ranna becomes the Meister."

"And he's got this crazy dog," I said. "Right?"

"Out of this world!" Karl replied, and laughed. I agreed. "It's surely out of yours, isn't it?" he added.

If at the back of my mind I had a Connecticut Yankee eager to rummage about in his own Middle Ages, was Ranna really as out of my world as I first thought? Hadn't I just agreed to lie freezing in this room, breathing the stench, waking to find a honeycomb of ice in my hair? The sound of water dripping into the court gave me a chill.

"I've got to run," said Karl, and off he went, swinging his backpack. I followed on his heels, down the way we had come up, passing the door where Madame's fire was crackling, then across the inner court, cleaned of most of its snow, and we both glanced skyward as we hugged the wall. Out on the ramp he gripped my hand, wished me a happy adventure, then marched under the archway and down through the orchard. Wood smoke had spread a soft blue veil over Muhldorf. I hadn't noticed, till that moment, the large church, with the onion dome, at the east rim of the plateau. A few houses huddled around it. Mountains rose behind it. I watched Karl, swinging his rucksack like a schoolboy, go along, with his crisp shadow beside him. If I was out of this world, what world was I in? I thought of Hans Castorp, up on his Magic Mountain, where the living would be better than it was at Ranna, but it seemed doubtful to me that his colleagues were stranger than Uncle James, the Meister, the dog Prince, and Antone, the father of his country. To keep the chill air off my chipped front tooth, I had to close my lips.

Five

S o began the winter I spent out of this world.

I lived at Schloss Ranna from early December until the first week of March, sawing wood, carrying water, shoveling snow, avoiding the Meister, helping Uncle James with his stamp collection, carrying the dog Dolly, in her foul-smelling basket, into the orchard where she would do her business, reading Madame's French novels, growing a moustache, spying on Mizi and the father of his country, and ceaselessly wondering what it was that made the Meister tick.

From the big alcove window, the winter sky gray as drizzle, the barren trees black, the snow without glare, like chalk on a blackboard, the mill wheel locked fast in the pond ice, it seemed to me that time, as I used to live it, had stopped. That what I saw before me was a snippet of time, cut from the moving reel, a specimen with more of a past than a future, a crack in time's door that I had my eye to, where no bird flew, no snow fell, no child played on the pond ice and no dog barked. To be out of this world was to be out of time. One day I liked it. The next day I thought I might go nuts.

A few days after Karl's return to Vienna, I was in the alcove, dropping pellets of bread dough to be gulped by the transparent goldfish. Feeling a chill draft blowing on my legs, I glanced up to see this fellow standing in the doorway. How describe him? He was like a living winter scarecrow. A mat of straw-colored hair, no hat. A broad flat face with eyes so small the light from the window didn't glint on them. He wore a sort of brindle home-spun, or it might have been burlap, that hung about him like a loose nightshirt, with strips of the same material wrapped about his legs below the knees. I had seen his like before in paintings. He dragged the sleeve of one arm across his face, spreading the shine of his nose drool like the track of a snail.

"Yes?" I said. That startled him. His brows went up, opening his eyes, and I saw his resemblance to Harry Lauder. He muttered something, but I didn't catch it. He turned away from me to lift a log from the pile, show me the sawed, powdery end. That was a pretty smart thing for him to do, and that was how we did most of our talking.

I was never clear what his name proved to be. I called

him Holz. I followed him through the kitchen, where we passed Mizi stooped over a tub, her backside broad as a chair back, down the stairs into the rear court, where a load of logs had just been dumped. The woodshed was right there to the left of the stairs, and in a clearing at the front they had this sawhorse. Holz took a crossbuck saw from a hook on the wall, and after a bit of bucking, on our first log, as to who was going to push and who was going to pull, we did all right. I was the better pusher. It was Holz's nature to pull. Two or three times a week he would come for me, and we would usually saw for about an hour. Holz didn't have a watch, or read the time on mine, but he had a sure sense of fifty-five minutes, and I think he would have loved a time clock.

My other chore with Holz was to carry a tub of water from the well to the kitchen. This tub was big enough for several kids to take a bath in, and full of water weighed—well, it weighed a lot. Two of the wooden staves were higher than the others, with a hole near the top through which a pipe could be inserted. Holz would be at one end, I would be at the other, with this tub full of water between us, slurping about as we carried it. In the old days, as I had seen it in paintings, the water had been cranked up in a moss-covered bucket, then carried about in jars on the heads of maidens, but the two of us worked a long-handled pump that first spilled the water into a length of rain gutter, from where it would run into our tub. Over the winter, to keep the pipe from freezing, they wrapped burlap and packed straw around it, and when we pumped the handle, bits and pieces of straw would fall into the rain gutter, then wash into the tub. Holz loved to pump, but with the first flow of the water he would stop to watch it spill into the tub. My feeling was he wanted proof that the pump was really working, but that wasn't it. One day I stood there with him, watching the pieces of yellow straw swim around in the water. Putting his big, chapped moon face toward me, he said, "Little fish maker!" and grinned like a pumpkin. It wasn't really clear to me if he was a bit of a poet or he thought they were fish. I often saw Mizi give Holz chunks of potatoes which he would gnaw on, like a carrot. She would sometimes wipe his runny nose with a wad of her apron, and if he happened to be stretched out asleep beside the stove she might stoop and stroke his matted hair, as she would a dog. These potatoes Holz gnawed were really for planting, not eating, with long green-tipped sprouts growing at the eyes, and if I had been a little bit surer of my German I would have told Mizi how I had once planted just such potato cuttings in Nebraska. But the word for potato, in German, is *Kartoffel,* which was exactly how I felt to pronounce it—Godawful.

However, I did have to ask her for some things. *"Gibt's heisses Wasser?"* I asked her.

She seemed to consider. "How hot?" she asked me.

"For shaving," I replied. Too late I saw that she had tricked me. Looking closely at my chin, she said, "Warm is enough!" and tested it with her finger. By the time I got the small pitcher of tepid water to my room, and some of it on my face, it was cold. That's the facts behind why I decided to grow a beard.

At the front of Schloss Ranna a long corridor connected the Meister's room on the east with the high-ceilinged music room on the west, warmed by the sun on those days we had any. The floor of this corridor tilted and dipped like those in amusement parks. Along it, at one point, was the water closet that everybody used over the winter. I tried to take a deep breath when I stepped into it, and do without breathing while I was there. On windy days a cold draft blew up it that puffed out my shirt and almost froze my bare bottom. Both Uncle James and the Meister used big flowered night pots that I had seen Mizi empty into the moats. Madame Deleglise also used a night pot, and I once saw it emptied from one of her windows into the court. Another time, when I was walking the dog, I heard this splash in the *Graben* behind me, and I thought of that painting of Brueghel showing people with their bottoms hanging out the windows.

Midway along this corridor, like a tight ship's cabin, was a small narrow room with two slotted windows in the outer wall. They were like portholes, but without glass, and burned like spotlights when the sun was on them. One wall of the room was lined with Madame Deleglise's French novels, in their yellow paper covers. There were also books in German, some Tauchnitz English editions, and three novels by Upton Sinclair, two of which I read. Beside a table strewn with old magazines and newspapers was a chair with dog or cat hairs matted on the cushion. Under some of the newspapers I found a fur-trimmed stereopticon viewer, with a cracked stereo view card in the holder, but when I tried to look at the card my breath fogged the lenses. I carried the viewer with me into the music room, where the sun had warmed the air in the alcove. What I saw was an Indian, his black hair in braids, wearing a white man's dinner jacket but his own buckskin trousers and beaded moccasins, and standing beside a short woman, her face blurred by movement, who held a small child. An elegantly dressed gentleman in a black coat and striped trousers had taken off his hat for the picture. His overexposed face had no features, but there was no mistaking Uncle James. So where was the Meister? He had taken the picture, and the woman holding the child was his wife.

That day the air in the music room had almost been warm. The windows faced the south, and if I stood close to the glass I could feel the sun's radiation. Just by enter-ing the room I had stirred up the air so that dust motes danced in the light beams. Except for the grand piano, on a low platform, the large room was empty. A dozen or so folding chairs were propped along one wall. The piano lid was raised, and several pieces of sheet music, curled and faded by the sun, were on the music rack. Ivories were missing from a lot of the keys, like bad teeth.

I could peer slantwise from the window into the deep blue of the *Graben,* the snow trampled by the deer, where a fellow with a head like corn in flower stroked the flank of one of the creatures he was feeding. Was this peasant and knave the father of his country? I thought it possible. How well his muscular hams filled the legs of his trousers. I sat in the warmth of the sun, thinking of California, where the new crop of oranges would be ripening, and some of the boys who were not going home for Christmas would be sneaking out of the dorms at night to fill their pillowcases with them. Real honest-to-God oranges, right there on the trees, with a skin you could peel like a banana. It was hard for me to believe that just the winter before I had done that myself. Now I was living in a castle with some pretty weird people, a herd of deer grazing in the dry moat below me. Nobody back where I had come from would believe it. I didn't believe it myself.

Sometimes I stopped to have a talk with Uncle James in his "office," a narrow room on the corridor that led out to the ramp. The only light came through a high slotted window, making a beam like a movie projector. Uncle James usually sat at his rolltop desk, in a chair that both swiveled and tilted. There he answered letters, kept accounts, wrote checks, mended his clothes—I often caught him with pins in his mouth, like a tailor—but mostly he filled out the order forms to be mailed to Sears, Roebuck in Chicago. The catalogue was customarily open there on his desk. The main problem—the others were minor—was that the items he ordered were usually out of stock, or if they weren't, the prices had altered. He had three letter files of typed correspondence dealing with this problem (he found the company scrupulous in all money matters), but nothing, no, *noth-*

ing, would persuade them to send him an up-to-date catalogue. The one on his desk was for the fall and winter of 1926.

Uncle James had his own kerosene-burning room heater, purchased in Brooklyn just before they had sailed, but after almost eight years of use the wick was so charred the flame no longer burned, and gave off a strong smell. Orders for hard candy and tobacco were lost in the mails, or the local postal people could smell them right through the wrapping. On the other hand, such staples as winter underwear, flannel shirts, bolts of cloth, nearly always came through after months of waiting. The postman in Spitz would make a special trip to Ranna on his bike in the summer, or by sledge in the winter, when he saw it was something from Sears, Roebuck. He was a friend of Uncle James, and they would have a schnapps and discuss the latest news.

One slightly warmer day I ran around taking snapshots. I climbed to the top of the tower, where Antone rang his *Jause* bell, and took shots of the courtyards, the deer in the *Graben,* and the way the walls spiraled out over the canyon, the view south toward Muhldorf, the view east toward Ober Muhldorf, and one of Uncle James standing out on the ramp waving to me. I also took a shot of Holz, holding the bucksaw, but when it was printed his face was a blank. I caught Antone by surprise, with his thumbs in his ears, wagging his big red mittens as he hooted at me. In another one he looked like Primo Carnera when he thrust his head forward for a close-up. I could see in his face it was his understanding that by

taking these pictures I got even with him. He didn't
resent it. He would get even with me as soon as more
snow collected on the roofs.

When Mizi saw me with my camera she covered her
head with her apron and ran for the kitchen, like a baby
hippo running for cover.

I got the Meister out on the ramp, from the rear. He
looked exactly like a small trained bear.

I caught Joseph in the courtyard, in his bloody
butcher's apron, his face beaming and happy, looking
exactly like Joseph.

Right when I had almost forgotten about Hermann
and Frau Unger, Joseph came for me, wearing his green
chauffeur's outfit, his cap with the cane sides, to ask if I
would like to go to Vienna. I wasn't sure. Going back to
Vienna would put in question all of my special feelings
about Ranna. It might ruin the whole thing. On the other
hand, I would soon have to pick up my English bike or
pay Frau Unger for another month's rent. A new renter
might use it or swipe it. The thought that I might lose it
decided my mind.

I put on my own shoes—I had been wearing a pair of
spike-soled mountain hikers, left by a guest the previous
summer—and trotted along behind Joseph to where the
car, the motor running, waited at the foot of the orchard.
The Meister was wrapped in blankets like a package in
the back seat. I took my place beside Joseph in the front.
I liked the little car, an Austrian Steyr, and it was none
of my business why the Meister was going to Vienna, so

I didn't ask. Soon enough I would learn why he had asked me to come along.

A light dry snow was falling in the canyon below Muhldorf, but Joseph had put on the chains, and the sky to the east seemed to be clearing. We crossed the Danube at Krems, instead of following the river, and headed for the main highway between Innsbruck and Vienna. It was snowing harder when we stopped at an inn to warm up. A guest with a chauffeur made quite a commotion and the natives left the bar to stand and gawk at us. Joseph sat at a separate table with a stein of beer, while we had mugs of chocolate. The natives looked about the same to me as the people around Ranna, with wooden-soled shoes, stained dark by the slush, burlap strips for leggings, and pale chap-smeared faces. They made me think of peasants in a Russian novel. Behind the men, a woman wrapped in a shawl stood holding a child like the beggars in Vienna. The Meister put a coin into the child's hand as we left.

A steady snow was falling, and it had darkened. We had our first problem, and I did my first pushing, when we had to steer around a big cart blocking the road. I pushed at the rear until I was dizzy, but the chains dug deeper ruts in the snow. The owner of the cart had unhitched his team and walked them over the rise, which left a broad trail for Joseph to follow and bring them back. During the time he was gone I would start the motor so the heater would warm up the car a little. When I glanced at the Meister he appeared to be asleep. On the floor at his feet he had two hot bricks; he had taken off his shoes to absorb the bloom of the warmth.

By the time Joseph returned with the farmer, and his team of horses, it was dusk. One of the horses was black, but in the falling snow he was easier to see than the white one. The farmer had had experience with automobiles and he was reluctant to hitch up his team to something that might attack them. On a recent occasion that had happened. Joseph stood for a long time in the snow, talking to him.

When we did get the two chains on the car, and the horses pulled us out of the ruts, the snow was so heavy on the windshield Joseph couldn't see where he was going. We had to let the horses drag us the half mile to the farmer's house, the rippling muscles in their broad backsides gleaming with sweat in the car lights. The house was like those in Muhldorf and Unter Ranna, with a wide-open stable on one side, open to the yard. In the stable he had an ox and a cow, their eyes shining like torches when they turned to stare at us.

Because of the darkness, and the snow still falling, it was decided we would spend the night with the farmer. I carried the two hot bricks, and the shoes the Meister had taken off, while Joseph carried the Meister into the house. Until he unwrapped him I think the farmer thought he was a sleeping child. While the bed was prepared for him, I sat on a bench at the table. At the back of the room, in a gable, I could see a thick covering of straw, but there was no sign of the kids I had seen in other houses. The whole room, in the dim light of the lamp, was like the dark brown chiaroscuro in Rembrandt's paintings. Joseph's shiny ruddy face was like that in a portrait, with highlights and gleaming colors, but the farmer's dark face was like a wad of soiled burlap. The lampglow added little luster to his small eyes. In the corner of the room, near the door to the stable, a woman with a shawl over her head moved pots around on the stove. It startled me to see, when she reached for a pot, her smooth plump white arm. A place was made for me to sleep on a cot near the stove, where I would be covered with one of the lap robes, and Joseph, on his own insistence, would sleep in the straw of the loft. He said that he preferred it, but nobody believed it but himself.

Until the woman brought a large bowl of soup to the table I had not seen her face. I sat there alone. No other eyes but mine beheld this heavenly vision. The shawl framed her face, her apple cheeks, the long lashes to her ice-blue eyes, and when her lips parted, I tell you, I saw the sweet vapor of her breath. Loose strands of her straw-colored hair were touched with gold.

"Bitte, bitte . . ." she said, like a normal creature, putting a bowl of steaming soup before me, but I could not speak. My mouth was dry. I saw the beat of the pulse at her white throat. Dazzled as I was, nevertheless I knew that this moment was fated. Here, where it was least expected, was the climax of my expectations. A creature beautiful beyond the telling of it, one I would woo (I had reserved the word for this occasion) and take back to California with me. (None of this, at the moment, presented problems, or dampened my elation.) How she would love it! How I would love her! From the window

of our cottage (I had one in mind) I would lean to pick
oranges and avocados.

Seated across from me, his chauffeur's hat on the
table, the top of his bald head damp with perspiration,
Joseph began the tale he had mastered concerning my
remarkable talents and background. Was she attentive?
Did she look at me, as I did her, with enthralled disbelief? Bundled up, as she was, it was hard for me to judge
all of her charms, but she was no Mizi. Normal arms
would easily go around her, lift her from the floor. A
flesh-and-blood person, nevertheless, with chapped
wrists and a blackened thumbnail on the hand that ladled
the soup. On and on Joseph babbled, cleaning his bowl
with a slice of bread. Later, like Hermann, he smoked a
cigarette of his own manufacture, the paper glowing like
a firecracker. The lamp was then taken from the table so
that beds could be made up elsewhere. The Meister lay
buried under bedclothes, the pants to his dark city suit
placed at the foot of the bed. From where I lay I could
see the glow of one cigarette, then another, then another, punctuated with his periodic snuffles. I could hear
the cattle shift their feet in the deep stable muck.

Never before, to my knowledge, had I known such a
delirium of emotion. Admittedly, I was short on experience. My unworthiness troubled me, but I would labor
to compensate for it. Did I sleep? Joseph pulled me to my
feet in the morning to drink hot milk from a mug. The
girl was gone. My breath smoked the chill air. Through
the door to the stable I could see the farmer forking
straw to his beasts.

Joseph went to fill the radiator with hot water while the Meister sat, like a beggar, gripping the mug of milk to warm his hands. He left several silver coins on the table, then shuffled down the path Joseph had cleared, to be rewrapped in the car. The windows were fogged with the air from the heater. Joseph cleaned the windshield with the sleeve and elbow of his jacket. The sky had cleared. The snow had settled so the road could be distinguished from the fields. When I glanced back, the farmer was standing like a bear hunter at the door to his house.

We sloshed along slowly to the main highway, then, the chains clattering, we were soon in Vienna. On Schottengasse, in front of the Studenten Klub, I was let out at the curb. At that time in the morning the peddlers had not set up their stands. I would not be returning to Ranna with Joseph because I had to take my bike to Ranna on the train. Did that concern the Meister? Did it cross his mind that I might not return?

"Look! Look!" he piped, putting up his hand. I looked and he said, "You aff mon-ee?" I wasn't sure that I had heard him correctly. "For fooooot! For train—you aff mon-ee?"

I reassured him that I had money. Through the window he gave me his grimace-like smile. Off they went, the chains slapping, through the arch to the inner *Stadt*. All this time I hadn't noticed that Joseph had put on, for adornment, a pair of clamp-type fireman's red earmuffs, the metal band concealed by his hat. They looked like carnations, and were as unexpected as the dream that had come toward me out of the shadows, with a steaming bowl of soup.

I was in Vienna, but my feet were not yet on the ground. I saw my friend Karl at the club, had lunch with Bogislav von Lindheim, then had a tearful parting with Frau Unger and Hermann before I carried my bike the four flights down to the street and rode it through the slushy snow to the station. Did it cross my mind that I just might take off and head for Italy? No, it didn't. I had these chores to do at Ranna. Holz and Antone would wonder where the devil I was, and there would be wood and water to carry. It was almost dusk when the train got to Spitz but I was able to walk the bike most of the way to Muhldorf. I thought I might drop dead on the road approaching Ranna, where I slipped back a step for every one I took forward, but Antone met me at the entrance to the stable with a basket of eggs and freshly churned butter. The way the spinning front wheel made the bike's light glow enchanted him. He carried the bike, I carried the basket, and walking up through the orchard toward Ranna we were both like the figures in Brueghel's painting of winter, returning from the hunt.

I'm reasonably sure all of this took place because the films of Holz and Antone I had asked Karl to have developed in Vienna he mailed back to me the next weekend. And in the walkway under the gable roof, where chinks of sky glittered between the shingles, my English bike with the Sturmey Archer gear was as real as the stench in my bedroom. It's hard to tell in a country with a place like Ranna where the real ends and the unreal begins, but these were the facts. I showed the pictures to Antone when I got them, and he laughed himself hoarse.

As a token of her high esteem for me, and her respect for Americans in general, Madame Deleglise—on those days when her dog, Dolly, seemed least disposed to use the ashes in her fireplace—trusted to me the transport of the old dog to where there was actually dirt to be scratched under the snow in the orchard. This was quite a little jaunt up and down the ramp. Dolly was not heavy, but she gave off a strong, acrid smell. When I made a clearing in the snow for her to stand in, she would just cower there, trembling, her feeble rear legs like those of a rabbit. It was up to me to kick a hole in the snow and turn up some real dirt. Then she had to sniff it, walk around and around it, crouch and whimper, do another turn around it, before she was ready to do her business. Sometimes nothing at all happened. "Let's get going!" I would say to her, but it was no help. She would look at me with her clouded eyes, then slobber and whimper until I scooped her up.

Back in Madame's room she would be fussed over, stroked and patted, given bits of goodies or a bone to gnaw on, just as if she had accomplished something. It wasn't my affair, so I kept what I knew to myself.

Sometimes Madame would have a fire crackling, the room so hot the windows were steamed over; other times she might be sitting up like a princess in the robes Russian women used to wear on sleigh rides, a fur hat on her head. Once I saw her with her hair so wild she looked like a shampooed poodle. We were both so startled we just stared at each other, as if the film had stopped.

Sometimes she might give me a piece of her Swiss chocolate, wrapped in silver or gold foil, or two or three of the little apples, the size of golf balls, that were usually reserved for compote. They were spongy to squeeze, and there was nothing much to them, but the apple scent would cling for days to my fingers. I didn't wash my hands often, the water not being handy, and my fingers would take on a shine like leather. I sometimes wondered if the Meister wet his hands at all, to avoid chapping, since it was Joseph who shaved him, and the only clean-looking spots on his hands were the fingers he used to roll the bread pellets.

The week before Christmas the two Deleglise boys came from school in Switzerland for the holiday season. I went along with the Meister to pick them up, in Innsbruck, which I thought was something special for me until we started back. What the Meister wanted, and got, was someone to help Joseph push the car out of the drifts. The car was a Steyr, made in Austria, with a boxy body like an Essex coach. The Meister and his two boys, wrapped up like parcels in thick lap robes, huddled in the rear seat, their feet on sacks of hot bricks, gabbling French at each other like schoolgirls. Their big entertainment was watching me get out and push. The snow thrown up by the spinning rear wheels soon worked its way down my collar and the back of my neck. Gobs of it plastered my face and my hair. The younger boy, Marcel, blond and pretty as a girl, had a shrill nasal voice and a girlish way of giggling.

In all my life I had never been with people who wouldn't help each other, when help was really needed. The idea of helping me didn't cross their minds. When I got back into the car, my face and hair caked with snow, they were red-faced and wheezing with laughter. Slouched between the two of them, as if he was being tickled, the Meister wore his familiar grin-like grimace, his eyes tightly closed. What tickled them all out of their minds was to see me climb out, hear the wheels spin and the chains clatter, then see me climb back in looking like a snowman. Every five or ten miles, sometimes less, I would have to go through that idiotic performance. I finally got so mad I yanked the rear door open and swore at them. This startled the boys so much they sat there open-mouthed, staring at me. I was prepared to let them have it. My blood was boiling, but in the winter silence, the metal pinging, the smell of the radiator alcohol like old times, I began to laugh. I had a fit of hooting laughter, leaning on the car, as if my maddening and accumulating fury was as much a part of laughter as it was of rage. When I couldn't seem to stop laughing, they laughed at me, all of them, including Joseph, who sat slapping his gloved hands on the steering wheel. If someone had come by right at that moment he would have known we were all drunk or crazy, which were the extremes of similar contradictions. Tears of laughter had given a shine to the Meister's shaved face.

I was the first to stop laughing, and as luck would have it, we got all the way to Muhldorf, on the slope below Ranna, before the wheels started spinning. At that point I got out, but instead of pushing I just took off and followed the road toward Ranna. From the archway at the entrance I looked back to see the three of them strung out behind me. The older boy, Jacques, was first, then the Meister, and lagging far behind them, Marcel, yelling at them in his shrill, complaining voice. Joseph had left the car to go to Ober Muhldorf for help. The whole crazy incident was fresh in my mind, the starts and stops along the road, the three of them hooting with laughter, but from where I was standing, at the entrance to Ranna, it no longer seemed so peculiar. I scooped a handful of snow and held it to my forehead to cool me off.

The next two or three days I was kept busy shoveling snow. I might see the blond head of Marcel at his mother's window, and hear her hoarse laughter at his witty comments. They took their meals in her room, but when a path had been cleared on the ramp they would come out and walk up and down before *Jause*. Madame always wore a black chinchilla coat, a Cossack-style fur hat, and carried a muff. Her voice in the open was crowlike and gruff, the contrary of Marcel's musical babble. He wore boots of patent leather, white fur gauntlets, with matching fur earmuffs. I saw his brother Jacques catch him in the courtyard, and dip his head into one of the snowdrifts, holding him there till he was red as a tomato. He would just stand there screaming until Mizi or Uncle James would come and lead him away.

One day I drove the car—Joseph was busy in the kitchen—towing Jacques on his new Christmas skis up the canyon to the high plateau from where we could see into Czechoslovakia. I strained to see in the landscape the characteristics I had noted in the Czech students at the club, a close-knit tribe, like the Finns, socializing only with each other. It did not cross my mind that these characteristics were in the language, not the landscape, and the great thing about having your own language was the way you could keep secrets, and remain private, before it became a way of communication.

On the way back to Ranna, most of it downhill, the Meister would yell at me to drive faster, and faster, so Jacques would have some bad spills. This gave him the same tearful exquisite pleasure I had given him pushing the car out of snowdrifts. Nothing personal. Just the pure unmitigated pleasure of seeing someone humiliated, made a fool of, squashed, but not quite demolished. I didn't like Jacques much, so I got more pleasure from his spills than his father. I didn't like his style, his dark, hostile manner, his rude, provoking way of speaking, slurring his French, and his superior, insolent, street-tough manner. He stopped being so hostile, however, the evening I beat him at Indian wrestling, where he thought he was good. Right away he was respectful and friendly with me, knowing I was his equal or better. I might have grown to almost like him, but the day after Christmas he was gone.

I was in the rear court with Holz, pumping water, when Marcel ran out of the corridor toward us, chased by Jacques. Marcel's coat flapped open: a white wool scarf, with long tassels, hung from his neck. As he ran by, he saw his beauty had impressed me, and he was pleased.

Jacques pursued him into the woodshed at the back of the court, then held him like a child as he stuffed handfuls of snow into his shirtfront and pants. Marcel shrieked and screamed but no one came to help him. When Jacques let him go he stood there howling, like a child in a tantrum, his brother standing off to one side, grinning at him. I didn't glance up to see, but I had the feeling that the Meister was at one of the upper windows, watching. Marcel was his mother's boy. It was just the sort of thing the Meister would hate to miss.

Just before Christmas, in the sunny music room, I sat reading Stendhal's *Le Rouge et le Noir*. I had looked up from the page to reflect on Julien's admission that he admired Madame de Rênal's looks but hated her for her beauty. That startled, pleased and confused me. Was it for this one read French novels? As I brooded on this dilemma, the Meister peered into the room to *psssst* at me, like a waiter. I followed him down the long corridor to his room, where he had been sorting good apples from bad. Spread out on his bed, they were all withered and spongy, with a strong musty odor, but some had a russet skin and looked less wormy than others. These he put in a sack and handed to me, but he carried a small sack of potatoes himself. We then walked back to the music room, where Joseph had started a fire in the blue-tile oven. The afterglow of the winter sunset filled the room with light. On the slope below Ranna, as if deep under water, I saw a dark file of figures emerging out of the canyon, all but a few of them carrying flickering candles. Drifting snow concealed parts of the trail and they moved along so slowly they appeared to be stationary.

I watched them come up through the orchard and follow the path that had been cleared on the ramp. They were kids mostly, without caps; their thatched blond hair made them look like goblins. All of them wore leggings of burlap, one coat sleeve dangling as if an arm was missing. A tall fellow, dressed like a schoolteacher, brought up the rear. As he passed beneath the alcove window I could see his breath smoke, his face white as a snowman.

Joseph led them up through Ranna, along the dark corridor and into the music room. If they could get their hands out of the long coat sleeves they received two spongy apples, two sprouting potatoes, and several pieces of hard Christmas candy, all of it from the Meister. Gathered in a clutter around the piano, they sang "*Stille Nacht, Heilige Nacht,*" the way it was probably sung in heaven. The tall young man who had come along with them gave a short speech of thanks, bowing low as he finished, then they all filed out through the door they had entered.

Some minutes later I saw them on the slope below Ranna, with their twinkling candles. Not to waste the fire in the oven, I stood close beside it, munching one of the apples. It occurred to me—with the time to think it over —that the Meister was a lot like Stendhal's Julien in the way he managed to surprise you. Stendhal would have liked him. They had more in common than just being French.

I might find soiled plates on the table in the morning, the fire in the stove a bed of ashes since nobody had banked it. I might find the kitchen warm, with nobody in it but Antone and Holz, asleep on the floor behind the stove. I took my supper in the kitchen, sometimes alone, sometimes with Joseph, Antone and Herr Zoller, who brought the eggs, butter and milk up from the stables. He took his long-stem pipe from his mouth when he ate; otherwise it was part of his face. He smoked a shredded yellow mixture like wood shavings, frequently blowing through the stem to keep it burning. In profile Antone's face was like the Indian on the buffalo nickel. Nobody talked. The glasses of cold green cider put everybody to sleep.

Snow collected on the roofs, in the inner and outer courts, making the carrying of wood and water difficult, and it was up to me to see that Dolly got to her scratch spot in the orchard. I stopped troubling with the basket, and the smelly cushions, and carried her whimpering and slobbering in my arms. She liked that. Sometimes she howled when I put her down. What she really wanted was the food she couldn't eat, having no teeth. At night Madame played opera music on her Victrola, all yelling and shouting, which I could hear if her fireplace smoked and her window stood open; I often missed it when it was quiet.

Once a month, weather permitting, Fräulein Schlepps came all the way from Spitz to take dictation and type business letters. I might see her red stocking cap and mittens as she mushed up the road from Muhldorf. Otherwise I would hear, in the silence of Ranna, the clack-clack of Uncle James's typewriter, an army-green Oliver that made me think of the drawbridges in Chicago. Fräulein Schlepps considered herself a big-city girl. She was pretty as a Kewpie, red-lipped, bob-haired, with big ice-blue eyes and a solemn expression, but her shoulders were thin, her figure straight and narrow as a clothespin. She wore a mat-black frock without frills or cuffs, the material flecked with typewriter erasures. Was it the long, cold walk to Ranna that gave her the feverish complexion? No, that she had always, along with her slight cough. The cough was not unusual among the young people since the war. When I met her she gave me her small, doll-like hand and said she was awed to meet me. It pleased her to practice her English on me. "How you do?" she would ask. "I do O.K." I told her about New York, the Empire State Building, and the oranges that

100

hung from the trees in California.

"Verstehen Sie?" Uncle James asked her. Solemnly, her small fist pressed to her lips, she would nod and cough.

As the snow accumulated, the work of restoration in the *Graben,* and on the bastille at the entrance, came to a halt. The buckets of rocks sat around humped with snow, or dangling from the ropes attached to winches. It all stopped like a clock, and would not be resumed until spring. Just as I was getting used to him, Beps went back to Krems. I watched him walk his motorcycle down the slope to Muhldorf, where I could hear the motor cough and sputter when he tried to start it. I liked him, I think, better than he did me, after I had beaten him at Indian wrestling. He couldn't accept that. He left early so we wouldn't have to say *Auf Wiedersehen.*

Sometimes the Meister would take his meals in his room and I wouldn't see him for three or four days. His room was narrow as a boat cabin, but with French doors in one wall that opened out on a view of the valley. He had a small wood-burning stove, named the Vulcan, that smoked most of the time because he wouldn't open the damper. Uncle James would often find the French doors thrown wide to air out the smoke.

The Meister's bed was attached to the wall, like a bunk, but so high off the floor he needed a stool to climb into it. Every night Mizi brought him hot bricks, wrapped in flannel, which she put between the sheets at the foot. He slept sitting up, propped by pillows, the way people do who read a lot at night. The day I was in his room he was reading an old copy of *The Nation,* and a recent copy of *Le Monde.* He didn't show me his room, but when I knew he wasn't there I had a look at it. In a wardrobe like the one in my room in Vienna he had a dark wool suit, a heavy dark overcoat, two white shirts on hangers, one tie, and a pair of oxfords with rubbers on them. What other clothes he had he was wearing.

I wrote a long letter to my sweetheart in California, who had gone to school in England and knew that people were peculiar, but after thinking it over I didn't mail it. It might lead her to think that I was the one who was crazy. Instead I sent her a postcard view of Schloss Ranna, painted in the eighteenth century, showing peasants at work and play in the orchard, and on it I wrote "Out of This World." Before I had a chance to mail it I smudged up the address and put it into one of the pockets of my suit coat.

That's how I happened to find out that I could hardly squeeze into my gabardine suit. The zipper would no longer close on the fly of the pants, and the coat that had hung loose on me would no longer button. Had six weeks of potato soup, *Butterbrot* and sawing wood done that to me? It had. All of those weeks I had been wearing some of the cast-off clothes left by guests who came out to Ranna over the summer, including sweaters and knickers I was happy to sleep in. How fat had I grown? There were no mirrors to tell me. In the glass of a bookcase I saw that my eyes were now small in my bearded face. Some of the money I had saved living at Ranna I would have to spend in Krems for clothes that would fit me, but I was pleased to look forward to a pair of the corduroy knickers I had seen on the smart young skiers in Innsbruck. Also a pair of the shoes made of one piece of leather, appropriate to a *Wandervogel* about to cycle in Italy on a four-speed English bike. With so much fat on my bones, I would save money by eating less.

We had a warm spell in February, with a lot of water dripping and running in the gutters. I was basking in the sun in one of the outer courts, where the Meister spotted me from a window. It pleased me to realize he had been looking for me.

"A ride! A ride!" he said. "Yes. We go for ride, I pool, yes?"

I didn't know what he had in mind, but I was game. I met him on the ramp, at the front, and we walked down through the orchard to the outbuildings that were part of Ranna, a lot of sheds and open lean-tos on a large open courtyard. I could hear pigs squealing and see chickens picking over the exposed manure in the stable. Two big, creamy oxen, with eyes like gods', watched me as if I were something special, straws sticking out of their mouths. There was also a small saddled reddish horse, and in the snow behind it a wooden-runner sled of the sort I had once had as a boy and never liked. All you could do with such a sled was haul laundry on it. There was no way to steer it, or run and belly flop with it. I watched the Meister fasten one end of the rope to his saddle, then he gave me the other, a knot looped at its end.

"You ride! You ride!" he said. "I pool!"

I got the idea. He led the horse into the open, on the road leading to Muhldorf, then stretched the rope out behind to where I stood with the sled. "You sit, I pool!" he said. To show me what he meant, he took a seat on the sled, took a grip on the rope, braced his feet on the curved runners. At that point I might have said, "*You* ride, *I* pool!" but actually I liked sleds better than horses. My last ride on a horse, I had been left on a tree branch along a gravel road between the farm and Nor-folk. So I sat down on the sled, took a grip on the rope, and waited for the Meister to mount the little horse. He took a lot of time cinching the saddle. Had he done this before? Most of the way to Muhldorf we went along at a walk while I tried to get the hang of steering the sled with my feet. It was not one of the thrill rides of my life, but some of the goblin-type kids came running out of Ober Ranna to watch us go by, and run along with us.

In Muhldorf, the fellow peeing on the porch of the inn greeted me with *Grüss Gott!* In the half hour or so since I had been sun-basking, the sky had clouded over, and a powdery snow was falling, prickling my face. In the canyon below Muhldorf the incline increased and the little horse began to canter. I was a good ten or fifteen yards to the rear, but the gobs of wet snow thrown up by his hooves began to fall on me. Some of them fell in my hair, like snow pies, and others splattered on my front. I had to use both hands to grip the rope, and it was hard to duck. When I did yell out for the Meister to stop, he didn't hear me. All I had to do was let go of the rope, but in that kind of situation it's the last thing you think of, and I've got this stubborn streak that makes me stick things out. The worse it is, the longer I'll stick. My feeling is—some fifty years later—that the Meister not only knew just what he was doing, he also knew me. I was one of those nuts like his son Jacques who would hang on until hell froze over—and it came close. Flakes of big snow plastered my face and sealed my eyes. I was steering the sled by the feel of the rope. I didn't even know when we reached the Danube and followed the highway into Spitz, since the snow concealed the river and I couldn't make out the dim lights at the inn. When the horse finally stopped I just sat there with this pancake of snow topping my head, and a bushel of it collected in my lap. Before the Meister looked to me he took care of his horse, which I could smell and hear wheezing, then, with a lantern, he came back to look at me. Did I look like something frozen in a cake of ice? He peeled off my snow topping, scooped the snow from my front, and that was it. Helped to my feet, I was on my own. I tailed along behind the Meister into the inn, where I stood beside the stove, thawing out and steaming, while he had a *Schokolade* and read the paper. To be fair, I have to say that he did ask me if I wanted anything, and of course I said no. The three or four men in the room, with their sad, gentle faces, their collarless shirts, were like those below the window of the club in Vienna, waiting to cluster around a peddler. They were like my friend Hermann with his rabbit eyes and bleeding gums. Little wonder that Antone was the father of his country.

When the time came to leave, and my hair was still wet, the barman loaned me a cap with earmuffs that smelled like manure, but I was glad to have it. It was dark but still snowing when we set off for Muhldorf, the Meister back on the horse while I walked along beside him, the little horse being too small for the two of us to ride. Here and there I saw the glow of a lamp, and heard dogs bark. My misery and self-pity were so great I didn't feel the cold much, or know how long it was before I left the Meister and his horse in the courtyard of the stable, and waded up through the orchard alone to Ranna, a gray hulk looming in the darkness. The dim bulb usually burning in Uncle James's small window was not visible. I used the broom on the landing to sweep off my shoes and pants, then went in, to find Uncle James asleep in a chair he had pulled up to the stove. He had taken off his shoes, and the air had the strong smell of his socks. I stood there beside him, still breathing so hoarsely nobody would guess I was almost bawling, my eyes blurred with tears.

Hearing shrieks in the kitchen, the sound of chairs scraping, I opened the door, to see Joseph pursuing Mizi, watch him catch her from behind and thump at her broad bottom with his hips. It seemed to me she didn't mind it too much.

Then he backed off, wheezing and laughing, to peer down at the butchered pig's tail sticking out of his fly like a corkscrew penis. He swaggered about in the light, showing it off, pulled it from his fly and tossed it into the bucket full of pig innards and scraps. Then they both went on about their work as if nothing had happened.

I didn't think that I had seen anything I shouldn't, but felt that something had ripped the veil to the past, just as I was passing, and I had seen through it.

At the window of the music room, my eyes creased against the sun glare, I saw in the *Graben* directly below me a bright patch of sunlight where the snow had melted. Drips from the roof honeycombed the snow. The line where the sun and the shadow overlapped quivered like a flame. On the bright side of that line I saw something strange.

First it looked to me like a mask, or shield, with a sort of putty-colored surface that crinkled. There were two small spots like widely spaced eyes, and centered, near the bottom, a small round hole or mouth. When my eyes had adjusted to the light I saw the forked brown legs, like a big insect. Now and then they moved, like butterfly wings. But the putty-colored object I had taken for a mask was the nude torso of the Meister, sunning himself. The two eyes were his nipples, and the hole was his belly button. His thin left arm lay across his face. He looked crumpled, as if he might have fallen from the sky, or the roof. When the sun left the wall, inching upward, he reached a handful of snow from the shadow and rubbed it hard on his chest and belly, then he rubbed some on his face. Just for a moment, as if he had told me, I saw what it was he liked about Indians. Then he got to his feet, buttoned up his clothes, and shuffled along the *Graben* bottom like a big trained rabbit. The feelings I had for such an odd little man in such a big strange place constricted my throat. I so wanted to like him, but he made it hard. At the top of the stairs that led up to the ramp he suddenly turned and looked right toward me. Did he see me, or just a reflection? If he saw me and thought that I had been spying on him it would have ruined the whole thing.

Knowing his watch does not run, I have stopped Antone to ask him the time. He lowered the barrow he was pushing, puffed like a dragon, and removed the timepiece from the bib of his overalls. Holding it to his ear, he listens, his eyes lidded. What he has heard reassures him. He considered the face, gave the stem several twists, then returned the watch to his bib. Whatever time it is, or will be, he has it safe inside the watch. In the glance he gives me I see that the joke is on me. I like Antone. His eyes tell me that I am the odd one. In the dark corridor to the music room I caught him, red-handed, gulping the spongy little apples, cores and all, snorfeling like a dog.

Forwarded from Vienna, a letter came from a fraternity brother in California. He had once asked me about Italy, and I had urged him to go there. But not with me. No one I had ever met seemed less a *Wandervogel*. He was big and shy, his hair already thinning, with a 1924 Model-T Ford coupe I used to borrow for dates. Himself, he didn't date. On spring weekends and over the summer, he helped his father grow avocados.

His letter said that if I would name the time, and the

place, he would meet me in Italy in March or April. Did I want to? We hardly knew each other. What I wanted more than the Alps, or the isles of Greece, or the white plume of Vesuvius, or the view of Naples, was to peel a bagful of oranges and lie on the beach with the sun in my face.

What time was it *really*? From Uncle James I found out we were in February, three days before Lincoln's birthday. A few days later, on the slope below Ranna, I saw another time I had failed to read correctly. With a shovel, someone had cleared away the snow to make a huge Nazi swastika:

卍

I had seen so few actual swastikas I didn't know the image was reversed. Thirty or forty feet square, it could be seen from Muhldorf if anyone was looking. A day or two later, fresh snow covered it up, but the depression in the snow revealed the pattern. Who had made it? One thing was certain: it took a shovel and a strong back.

I wrote my fraternity friend in California that it was hard for me to make plans for the future, living as I was in the Middle Ages, but I would try to be in Trieste, Italy, the second week of March, at the American Express office.

From Genoa, Italy, I had a postcard from Karl. He was soon leaving for Buenos Aires, where he invited me to pay him a visit. I would find him at his father's fabric business. He wished me a *gute Reise* in Italy, and much

109

success as a writer. That astonished and pleased me. What ever led him to think I might be a writer? But it seemed more plausible to me now that I had a moustache. (The beard would be shaved off.) Italy called to me, Buenos Aires called, but it snowed steadily at Ranna, filling the courts and the cracks between the planks on the floor of my room.

The night Joseph woke me up, I'd been asleep for some time. His shiny bald head loomed above me like the moon lit up from the back side. A milky moonlight filled the windows.

"Was gibt's?" I asked.

"Excuse me!" he said. I excused him. "The hunt! The hunt!" he said, his hushed voice urgent. He was in his chauffeur's coat and riding breeches. In the crook of his arm the barrel of a gun glistened. He waved his hand to the windows, but I did not feel urgent. I was a reader, a dreamer, not a hunter. *"Schnell!"* he said, giving me a shake, and I got up.

Something to wake me would have helped, but we did not stop at the kitchen. Our shoes rang like iron on the corridor cobbles. Out on the ramp was Antone, his hams tight in his britches, and a long coat draped the figure of Holz. He might have been sleepwalking. No features showed in his face. Antone led us off, his hair up like a scarecrow, then Joseph, with the light glinting on the gun barrel. Holz shuffled in a trance of cold at the rear. A vapor hovered about us from our own breathing, like leaks from a radiator, the snow under our feet brittle as glass.

Down we went through the orchard toward Ober Muhldorf, where a dark clump of figures waited. They were beaters. I had heard about them. They preceded the hunters, yelling and hooting, stirring up the creatures crouched in the field stubble. Softly Joseph called out, "Hallo, hallo?"

Owl-like came the answer: "Hal-looooo, hal-looooo." One of the beaters, who held a lantern, waved it, the flame hardly visible in the shimmering brightness. Now we made our approach. In a hush of muttering and white vapor the beaters huddled, shuffling their feet. Among the hunters I noted a jolly fellow with knickers, a tuft of fur at his hatband, high two-buckle galoshes. We beaters strung ourselves out in a row facing the furrowed rows of stubble. The crispness of the shadows made it confusing. Everything moved. We stood silent, shifting from foot to foot, waiting for the Big Hunter to give the signal. The four hunters had skirted the open field to a position where trees grew out of the gully. There, in concealment, they would await the rabbits. Two of the hunters were from Unter Ranna. I saw that we numbered eleven beaters, with perhaps three or four yards between each of us. His mittens cupped to his beaming face, Antone honked like a river steamer. He was silenced. But even the hunters understood about Antone. At the signal, the far hoot of an owl, the beaters flailed their arms, slapped their hands on their thighs, barked, howled, and stamped their feet as they marched. That part of it I liked, and it warmed me up.

I made a good beater. I had had some experience

hooting and howling like an Indian, and my lungs were strong. Hearing me, any rabbit, or anything else, would have run for its life. We all kept up this racket for the time it took to walk from the road to the edge of the gully. I had seen nothing. But the excitement and cold had filmed my eyes, and my head buzzed. Nothing had prepared me for what then happened. The explosion of the guns, a split second apart, in spite of the great clatter we were making, splintered and demolished the great globe of the sky. The echoing thunder went up, then down, the canyons, bounced off the mountains, so that I stood with my eyes closed tight, my head lowered. All of my companions ran, some of them falling, to the point where the trees began and the hunters were gathered, gesticulating. They were fighting, surely, over the slaughter of rabbits! We all formed a panting, wheezing circle around them. Joseph pointed to where the rabbit had come from, and to the spot at his feet, where he had shot it. All were agreed. All had done the same. There at his feet. A space was cleared at the center to look for the tracks, but with all the commotion, they had been obliterated. One fact was certain, though. Joseph waited for silence to make it. The rabbit had been seen, the rabbit had been shot, and then disappeared. Anyone could see that he was not there. Nor were there tracks indicating that he had escaped. None. On the wide, gleaming moonlit slope, not the single track of a rabbit. *Unglaublich. Fabelhaft. Ausserordentlich.* Out of this world. In this pregnant pause, Holz had turned from us to pee in the snow.

The hunter from Ober Muhldorf, with the fur on his

hat, invited hunters and beaters to his house to celebrate the occasion, but Joseph, looking before and behind him, glancing up the slope at the walls of Ranna, and down the slope to the roofs of Muhldorf, regretted that Herr Morris, a guest in their midst, one who had come from a world where no snow fell, was surely exhausted by the night's events and eager for the shelter Ranna provided. All eyes gazed at me, but saw little. I sucked the bitter air through a muffler concealing my face. As we departed, Antone, cupping his mittens to his face, cried out, *Hallo, hallo. Radio Wien!* like the Vienna radio announcer. There was no comment. Antone was even better known for other works.

We walked single file in the tracks we had made coming down. Deep gulps of the air burned my lungs. We paused frequently to wait for Holz. The moon shimmered like a reflection on water. No stars anywhere. To myself I said that this was what was meant by the white nights of Russia. All around us the snow glittered like Christmas tinsel.

I stopped in the dining *Saal* to thaw my cold feet, then went up the snow-sprinkled stairs to my room. Under Madame's door I saw the flicker of fire. Hearing my steps, the old dog whimpered. In the room with the trophies, their glass eyes shining, the sheet-covered furniture appeared to be concealed by mounds of snow.

If Madame Deleglise was in a bad mood she would not let Mizi carry food into her room. It would be left on a tray at the door, and that was where they would find the dirty dishes. After I had carried Dolly to her spot in the orchard, I would leave her at the door, and knock. This time, when I knocked, she called, "Gom een! Gom een!" I went in. A log smoldered on a high mound of ashes, the air was blue with smoke. I turned to leave, but she cried, "No, no—gom een!" She reclined on a bed with a yellow comforter, propped up in a nest of cushions. A ribboned nightcap, with a puffed crown, sat on her head, like the big bad wolf in "Little Red Riding Hood." "Ow you like Ranna?" she asked me.

"Very much," I replied. Too late, I saw it was a loaded question. Her dark face clouded. She muttered several hissing curses.

"You like? You know why you like? You are nod a preez-nur. I am a preez-nur!" Her chubby hands slapped the comforter, stirring up a cloud of dust. "A preez-nur! A preez-nur!" she cried. "You hear me?" We both looked about the large room. It would have been ideal for the Prisoner of Zenda. One high-gabled window, several that were slotted, the rafters in the peaked ceiling black with wood smoke. "Gom here!" she barked at me, beckoning me closer, and I obeyed. She tilted forward to see me more closely, her hands placed dramatically on her bosom. She had more of a talent than I had suspected, and remarkable eyes. Captive in her dark tower, on a bed strewn with French novels, she perceived me as straw thrown on her fire. Her fists clenched. She turned to pull on a cord that hung at her side, and I heard the bell sound in the kitchen. Did she mean to have Mizi throw me out? I thought her capable. I was out on the

114

stairs, headed down, as she passed me going up, a smear of flour on her cheek, a lace of suds drying on her plump arms. If only her almond eyes had given me the assurance that I, too, was a *preez-nur,* but she didn't, and little she seemed to care.

Joseph had found me reading in the library annex, where I had found a Baedeker of Italy and was engrossed in the maps. What Joseph had to say to me, being novel, I did not understand. He beckoned me to follow him, and we went below to the office of Uncle James. He sat at his desk soaking stamps from the envelopes of his recent correspondence. His muffler was twisted about where his neck might have been, and his lips were shiny with the syrup of a horehound drop from Cedar Rapids. He did not appreciate the interruption, Joseph explained.

"Beek peek hass leedle peex," said Uncle James.

What did that have to do with me?

"Mutter peek"—he spread wide his arms—"roll on leedle peex. You sit and watch."

"Where?" I asked. Joseph explained. The mother pig and her new litter were at home with Herr Zoller, where they should be. Joseph would show me. I lacked experience baby-sitting little peex, but Uncle James reassured me. "Iss nutting," he said, and smiled to see them all before him. "Besides, iss varm! For leedle peex haus muss be varm!"

Joseph led me off. Already spots of green were showing in the orchard where the snow had melted. Also black ruts in the road leading to Muhldorf. In the courtyard of the stable, water sat in puddles. Were mother pigs knowledgeable in such matters? Had she timed it for spring? In the shed we passed through were the oxen, their great creamy bodies like mythical beasts. A woman opened the door, a wad of the babushka that circled her head held to her mouth. The room we entered was large, lit by lamps, the stone floor strewn with straw. At the back of the room a loft, the rafters covered with straw, with several goblin-eyed small fry staring at me. I looked at them for some resemblance to Antone. In one corner of the room a great pink and white sow sprawled on her side on a bed of hay, a squirming mass of mini-piglets tugging at her teats. They were pink and hairless as baby mice, with tiny cloven feet. The sow's eyes were lidded by long thick blond lashes. She grunted softly, like a happy dreamer, stirring bits of chaff. What did I think of? I thought of Mizi. The Lord of life would have to forgive me. Here was contentment that exceeded expectations, even mine.

A three-legged stool sat at the rim of the straw, with a pole that could be used to push or pull a piglet. There I would sit. I heard but followed little the instructions Joseph gave me. Was there a problem? There was a problem when the mother sow changed her position, rolled on her bed. Not through lack of affection, nor because she was careless, but sheer bulk complicated matters. Thirteen piglets—Joseph paused to count them —keeping the count at thirteen was the problem, since one or more was inclined to scoot under or behind her.

And that would be one less. Nor was it just the loss of a piglet, but in time a pig. Frau Zoller was a woman with much work to be done, and her children were too small for piglet watchers. A man was needed. Strange as I might be, I was a man.

I litter-sat for two days and one long night. Was it possible to feel tender and fraternal affections for a sow? I felt them. It also reassured *her* that I felt them. Often she would lift her head, with its purse-size ears, and gaze at me through her long blond lashes. Oink, oink, she would say to me. Oink, I said to her. Sometimes she would snort, clearing away the floor chaff, or use her snout like a nozzle to suck up food scraps. Her brood seemed to be an immaculate conception. The bolder ones came closer to sniff me over, their little hooves like the handles of pocket knives. If I grabbed a piglet it was like a moist football. How it squealed. In moments of rebellion, weary of their greedy sucking, the mother sow would labor to her feet, with half the brood dangling like pig pods. She looked to me for help, and she got it. I would use the pole to pry them off her teats, like so many huge leeches. At night I often saw mice playing in the straw, and the flick of their shadows at the edge of the litter. Both considered me another hog, but a strange one. Twice daily I was fed a soup of gruel and milk in which pieces of blood sausage floated. Pig blood. I slurped it down and smacked my lips. On the third morning a girl, as big and strapping as Mizi, but her broad face puffy and her nose chapped, took my place. I'm afraid I greeted her with some resentment. Did she think she

117

could take *my* place in the sow's affections? Her name was Rota Dinge. Her wooden-soled shoes, soaked dark by the slush, were sniffed by the piglets while she was napping, which she did most of the time.

The snow was melting again, and I could hear it drip and gurgle at night. On what I took to be a Sunday, or a holiday, Madame Deleglise came to dinner dressed like one of the Three Musketeers, or Cyrano de Bergerac. A large hat with a plume, the brim turned up on one side, added about eight inches to her height at the table. Purple velvet pantaloons were tucked into black leather boots, gold- and silver-looking chains dangled into her lap. It had to do with some role she had sung in opera, and what it did for her spirits was remarkable. Her eyes flashed, she roared with hoarse laughter. The cloud of her perfume hovered over the table. After bowls of soup, in which dumplings were floating, Joseph entered the room with a platter that required we clear a space at the center of the table. We all shared in the excitement. Uncle James rubbed his palms together like an Indian making fire. The platter was lowered to the table, and there before my eyes, steaming like a baked apple, was a roast suckling piglet! One of my piglets! Uncle James rose from his chair to do the carving with a large blade that Joseph had just sharpened. I rose with him. Perhaps only Joseph, who looked at me with surprise, was aware that I had left. From the landing on the stairs I whooped up the dumplings, and felt the weakness in my loins, a word I treasured. If Mizi had seen me I would have died.

I made my way across the court to Uncle James's office, where, some hours later, he found me still resting, my eyes to the wall to avoid the look of heavenly contentment on his grease-smeared face.

After several days of spring-like weather, the air in my room was warmer but I couldn't breathe it. I asked Joseph about it, and I saw that he knew it well. Would it continue? I asked him. It would. How long? Until the pit at the foot of the latrine was emptied. And who was it that would do the emptying? We would. Joseph often found the questions that I asked him puzzling.

That was one thing. A sledgeload of freshly sawed logs dumped at the foot of the orchard was another. Why there? The problem had a history. For three or four generations, that was where the log supplier had dumped them. At the foot of the orchard. So that was where they were dumped.

The ground was too soft and mushy for a wheelbarrow, so those logs would be carried, an armful at a time, the quarter mile from the stable into the rear court, where they would then be sawed into smaller pieces. More than two cords of fragrant, wet, unseasoned, heavy wood.

So what we did was improvise a stretcher, made up of saplings, to carry four or five logs between us from the foot of the orchard to the woodshed in the court. This stretcher of logs could not be lowered, or shifted, until we reached our destination. The chapped hands of Holz, in their ragged mittens, endured this burden like hooks.

After two trips my hands were blistered. I could not shape a fist, or slip them into my pockets. A day later I managed to twist my ankle. My collapse on the ramp, very dramatically timed, got me considerable attention. My arm around Joseph's shoulders, his around my waist, I hobbled to the couch in Uncle James's office. Unfortunately, I had not foreseen that snow would be applied to reduce the swelling. I thought my foot would freeze. I was still there in the morning when the mail came up from Muhldorf, with a letter from my friend in California. He was sailing from New York to Genoa, Italy. He planned to meet me, as we planned, in Trieste. Amazing how the snow had improved my ankle in just one night! I still hobbled a bit—not of much help in the carrying of logs and water—but in a few days surely, and on a bicycle with gears to smooth out the rises, and with spring, so to speak, just around the corner, or already arriving in the Bay of Naples . . . ! When I spoke to the Meister, who had lived in Italy, who had indeed hiked in the hills above Florence, and rested in the gardens of I Tatti, he advised me that I might find Italy on the cool side in March.

Uncle James was more sympathetic. Did I think he didn't know what was "eating me"? Had he not himself been young in Vienna, and for almost three weeks on Lake Como, near Bellagio? *"Ein viertel Frühling!"* he sang. *"Ein viertel Wein, ein viertel Liebe, verliebt muss man sein!"* He broke off to recall a summer night in Verona, where Madame had performed to a standing ovation. For himself, he found the *jeunes filles* on the plump side, and well chaperoned.

It was not for the girls I went to Italy, I replied, already having a not-too-plump girl friend in California, to which news he arched his hairless eyebrows, his wide mouth contracting to a kisser's moist pucker.

Antone, the father of his country, gripped and shook my hand, then left me holding his fingerless red mitten. I had meant to give him my Magic Match, a metal nail that would strike and burn, but his prank gave him much more pleasure. At the end of the corridor, framed against the winter sky, he stood with his legs spread wide like the Jolly Green Giant, a fire in his yellow hair.

Joseph asked if I would send him a postcard from California.

Holz lay asleep behind the stove, so I didn't wake him.

Uncle James asked me not to forget him, and I didn't.

Mizi was nowhere that I looked. Nowhere.

I made my getaway. I was halfway down the ramp when the Meister called to me. The French doors to his room stood open, he basked in the sun. He waved, and I could see flecks of red in his week-old beard. Mizi came out of the room at his back to thump the head of her dust mop on the wall. She had a pale-blue dustcloth pinned to her hair, and as I waved to her she put one hand to her face, covering her mouth. Did I or didn't I hear a suppressed shriek of laughter? For a moment her broad back filled the opening, then she was gone. A big cow of a girl, really, who just happened to have a creamy complexion and the slanted eyes of women from the steppes of Russia. I was leaving just in time, I told myself, before something unforeseen might happen, and whoever

121

might prove to be the father of the country, it wouldn't be me.

I had to carry my bike all the way to Muhldorf, the road to Ranna chewed up by the tire chains. Below Muhldorf there were lanes where the snow had melted, and I could ride. Once I got on the bike I was seized with an impulse to pedal like mad. At the foot of the canyon, seeing the Danube as muddy as the Missouri at Omaha, I felt a weakness like that at losing a sweetheart.

Uncle James had assured me that the barber in Spitz would not be offended by my long dirty hair, or my scraggly soft beard. I found his shop empty; he was seated in the chair, reinforcing the buttons on his vest. He greatly admired my long silken moustache, which reminded him of Franz Josef, often seen in Spitz before the Great War. He washed my mane of hair, wrapped it in towels, and on the heel of his hand, as he shaved me, I saw the glint of copper-colored hairs in the lather. Tilted erect, and fanned by a towel, I saw in the mirror he held before me the flushed, full-jowled face of a stranger with wavy brown hair. I was able to persuade him to go easy with the clippers. Where I was going, I said, longer hair was in fashion. And where was that? I rolled my eyes. I mentioned Capri and the Bay of Naples. He looked at me with the eyes of Hermann on first beholding my Sturmey Archer gear. Would I welcome, he asked me, a suggestion? It proved to be a touch of wax to the ends of my moustache. Whose face was it? I tried to recall if Gustav Aschenbach looked a bit roguish. To this barber shave—my first and last—I owed the impression that I was a new man. How well I understood, as he whisked me off, the compliments he gave me about the view from the rear.

Six

*B*ogislav von Lindheim, paler and thinner than
usual, his plus-fours tucked into the tops of his
unbuckled galoshes, knew that I had been away, somewhere, but he had forgotten where. As we sat in the
alcove window, overlooking Schottengasse, a ragtag
company of Austrian soliders with knapsacks, canteens,
and rifles with bayonets marched by in broken ranks
below us. I thought it had to be a movie. Bogislav was
not amused. Chancellor Dollfuss, single-handed, was
trying to unite the country. An American girl from
Cleveland, in a fur-trimmed tweed skirt and jacket, her
Lucky Strikes in a tin of flat fifties, had taken my place
as the voice of the new world. She gave parties in her
Ringstrasse apartment and sometimes arrived at the
club in a taxi. Had I known that Pius Michael Prutscher

had been very keen on Catherine White? No, I had not known.

The night train from Vienna got me to the Italian border, high in the Alps, just at daylight. Along the way, as the train rose into the mountains, I watched the big, moth-like snowflakes falling like ashes about the hooded station lights. The long screeching climb, the starting and stopping, the clackety-clack of the wheels in the tunnels, was like the trip of Hans Castorp, rising from the flat plains into the mountains. I wore the new hiking clothes I had bought in Krems: the wide-wale plus-fours, a sweat shirt with a zipper collar, a leather jacket with tassels on the pocket zippers, and shoes made of a single piece of leather in the prison south of the Danube. There was still wax on the tips of my moustache. The three young skiers in the compartment with me studied my outfit and me with interest. Was I an *Ausländer?* I was. I would surely have no problems, they assured me, since I spoke such excellent German. They had been to Italy. The roads of Italy were used by more German *Wandervögel* than Italians. *Auf Wiedersehen!* we all said.

At the border the Italian officials were puzzled to examine my passport. Americans did not look as I did, or appear at the top of the Alps with *biciclettas.* I was taken in hand, and sat with two border guards, waiting for the border official. A small white-haired man, with beautiful manners, a black cape about his shoulders, he did not believe me for a moment, but he liked me. Had I *really* come from California? Was I an artist? He shared my excitement to be entering Italy. He, too, was an artist, he had once been young, and he felt moved to be generous.

Outside the depot it snowed. The official embraced me as we parted, and I carried my bike through the slush of Tarvisio, down the narrow road beyond it, the high air burning my lungs, my eyes blurred with cold. I was low on oxygen, but high on exhilaration. I was in Italy! The air that I breathed, the snow that fell on me, the road beneath the snow, were all Italian. I plowed ahead. I seemed to have all of it to myself. The snow let up, the road tilted downward, and where the snow thawed I was able to ride. Down, down I went, the snow thinned and disappeared, the road followed a widening, boulder-strewn river, the water running white in the narrow channels, down, down I went, through villages gray as granite, through blowing wisps of cloud, through sheets of drizzle, with the air blowing warmer and warmer, down, down into a wide river basin with the smoke of factories and the racket of traffic.

I had not eaten since the day before, but I was too excited and elated to stop. The landscape opening around me was like that of California, the mountains rising abruptly, the canyons of boulders fanning out to spread on the arid wash, but I saw it all with shining eyes. I felt nothing but a buoyant elation. A hundred or more kilometers from where I had started, I came out on a plain, with stony fields and cypress trees, the bell towers rising from clumps of trees and houses, and in the outskirts of a sprawling town I pulled over to the curb to ask where I was. My ears were ringing. A large woman, dark as an Arab, looked up from sweeping the sidewalk to smile at me. Did I smile in return? Painless as a lover's swoon, I collapsed at her feet.

I had skillfully managed to faint dead away just a few yards from a hostel, and had been put to bed in a small, comfortable room. I slept through the rest of that day, the night, and until late the next afternoon. A young girl, with coppery blond hair, brought me a thick vegetable soup and hard white rolls. When I finished she brought me a second. That I could eat and talk seemed to amaze her. An Italian policeman came to check me over, and compare my face with the one in the passport. Alas, they no longer matched. This led to much laughter. Two older women were called in to discuss this problem, and one of them perceived the person behind the moustache. My moustache was stroked and pulled to verify it was real. There were no chairs in the room, so they all stood together, like people at a party, in a fever of delight, suspicion and disbelief. After my winter at Ranna, I felt right at home. Was there anything I wanted? I said I wanted to *dormire.* How it pleased them to understand me. To sleep, of course. I wanted to sleep. They left me in a hush of quiet, the room already darkening. My head was spinning with the flood of impressions, and the need to reflect on all that had happened, but the next thing I knew, light flooded the room, and I was awake. What I thought to be a brawl in an adjoining room proved to be two men greeting each other in the hall.

In one day's frenzied pedaling, most of it downhill, I

had come almost two hundred kilometers. That seemed hardly possible, but I had done it. It helped to explain my swooning collapse. My motor had run out of fuel, and the machine had stopped.

I was in Italy, but the wind off the mountains, sweeping the plain toward the sea, made my ears buzz and tingle. The cold, sunless light was like the pallor of the natives. If I stopped in a square, for something to eat or drink, a pack of boys in knee britches soon surrounded me and my bike. They had never seen one like it. They had to toot the horn and work the gears. Most of them had the lean, black-haired good looks of the boys I had known at the Y in Chicago. It made me shiver to see their bare thin legs, their knees blue with cold.

With the wind at my back I made good time, but I was always getting lost. All the natives knew where they were going, and had no need of signs to tell them. Where the sea was up ahead, so close I could smell it, I stopped at an *albergo,* the space in front crowded with trucks and wagons. Inside, a lot of Italian men were eating and playing cards. I took a seat at one of the large tables, and had a meal of *polenta,* a warm slab of corn-meal mush, served without butter or syrup. I gulped it down, and drank a glass of red wine. I would have liked to sit there, absorbing the smoke and the racket, but I couldn't keep my eyes open. A little girl with long braids led me up-stairs to a cell-like room, the opening at the top covered with chicken wire. When I sat on the bed to take off my shoes, my head thumped the wall. The sheets had been slept in, but not often. I could hear men coughing and snoring around me, and one who sang to himself, softly. Over and over he sang the same refrain until I fell asleep.

So close by I marveled that I hadn't heard it was the sea. There was no beach or waves to speak of, just rocks and a frothy, dirty foam, like dishwater. It was hard for me to believe this was Homer's wine-dark sea. It looked more impressive from the road approaching Trieste, cut into the sheer side of the cliff, with the sea breaking below it, but even that was nothing to compare with the cliffs at Big Sur, near Carmel, and the cypress and the sea at Point Lobos. What would the Greeks have done if they had had a coast like California?

In Trieste I went straight to American Express, where there was no mail for me, nor any message from my friend, so I came out to stand at the front with an American girl from Ann Arbor. *Tant pis,* she said to me. She was waiting for her mother to take her by car to Ljubljana. I had never heard of Ljubljana, or why a pretty girl would want to go there. If you're accustomed to a campus crowded with American girls, especially if it happens to be in California, there's so many of them you tend to forget that there is much special about them. I didn't even think to ask her her name. As she walked away it struck me—it didn't just occur to me, because I had read it somewhere—that having to settle on just one girl, considering all the girls there were, was really one hell of a problem. I only knew a dozen or so by their first names, and I was already perplexed.

As this girl walked away—she turned once to wave at me—I saw a big fellow in a rumpled blue serge suit, a beret on his head, riding toward me on a bike with the front wheel so warped it wobbled and rubbed on the fork. The seat of the bike was too low for his long legs, and riding it wasn't something that he was at ease with. One leg of his trousers was rolled up to the calf to keep it from dragging on the chain. Until he waved at me, and smiled, I didn't know it was Lorne.

I had my reservations, but I was so glad to see his big, friendly face that I went toward him and threw my arms around him. That surprised him, since we had never been close, but I'd already been six months in Europe and felt lonelier than he did. In the few years I had known him, he'd had the habit of running one hand through his hair as if he feared he might lose it, and it was already thinner than I remembered. I was so damn glad to see him I probably talked too much. It just hadn't occurred to me, until I saw him, a big American in a blue serge suit, riding a cheap Italian bike with the wheels warped, how different Italy would be without him. When he had a chance to say something, he said, "Well, I made it, but it wasn't easy." That was a pretty long speech for him, and it was one I liked.

It rained for three or four days, maybe longer. We found a warm place to sleep, with clean sheets, in a public hostel, a big whitewashed room, the beds against the walls. If we sat up in bed we faced the person in the bed across the room. There were seldom more than two or three of the beds occupied, besides our own. In the bed directly across from me, day and night, was Professor Gianelli, from Gorizia. I saw the name in a book he had loaned me, with pictures ridiculing Mussolini. Professor Gianelli came to Trieste to rest, and refresh his mind. He had brought with him a suitcase full of books, and a duffel bag of small oranges. Now and then I saw him munching a piece of bread, but he *lived* on oranges. Every time he peeled an orange the sweet fragrance of the peel filled the room. He looked imposing in the bed, with his big, craggy head and topknot of white hair, but I never saw him standing up. He was a teacher all right, accustomed to lecturing, and gesticulated like an actor when he talked, the sleeves of his long yellow underwear pushed back on his bony, sallow arms. He read most of the night. If what he read got him excited, he would wake us up to talk about it. We understood little of his speech, but it was easy to guess at what he meant to say. He had this rage about Mussolini, but he would never actually mention his name. He would make a face, spreading his mouth wide with his fingers, or he would make the gesture of a knife slicing his throat, accompanied by a sound like a sheet tearing. The sound really disturbed me, like watching someone suck on a lemon.

Although he had come to Trieste to read and relax, having us to lecture to got him excited, and confused his plans. He read aloud to us the passage he might be reading, along with what he considered helpful comments. It worried me the way he heaped abuse on Il Duce, about whom I knew little or nothing, but the two other Italians, one with a kidney problem, listened with indifference or ignored him. One was a plump, moon-faced man who pressed his suit pants nightly under the mattress. That seemed to me very funny. Something that Chaplin or Keaton might do preparatory to spending the night in the gutter. He never said a word. He never looked to me to say anything.

One day we went to the city art museum, one of the places we could go to get out of the rain, where I saw a large mural-size painting of young people listening to music in a darkened room. They were sprawled in chairs, or reclining on a couch, and one of them, a beautiful young woman, her head resting on her interlaced fingers, seemed to gaze from the painting directly into my eyes. Her auburn hair was worn in the style of the nineties, swept up from her ears and the nape of her neck, and I was filled with an aching longing to listen to the music she was hearing. Was it too late for me to learn to play the piano, the violin? What did riding a bike around in a freezing rain have to do with love, beauty and depth of feeling? As we left the museum I happened to notice the guard dozing at the door. He was the plump, moon-faced man who pressed his pants under the mattress, and the inaudible music I had found so moving had put him to sleep.

We had our big daily meal at a café frequented by laborers and miners. The miners sat together, wearing their hats with the lamps, the whites of their eyes shining in their soot-blackened faces. The woman who sliced the *polenta* did it with a piece of string tied to one finger of each hand. This cut it quicker and cleaner than a knife. Neither of us liked it too much, but it was filling.

One day one of the miners seated near our table spoke to me in English. Were we Americans? We were. While

132

he ate, that seemed to satisfy his curiosity. Later I offered him a cigarette, which he inhaled deeply, closing his eyes. He liked American cigarettes. He had lived for several years in America. Where? I asked him. In Utah. He had worked in a silver mine in Utah. He liked American movies. He had gone to movies every Saturday night. He had been part of a crew to work in the mines, and then he had been shipped back to Trieste. He was not Italian. He was a Jugoslav. Nor did it please him to think I thought so. When I shook his hand to say goodbye, he said to me, "So long."

I hadn't troubled to study Italian, thinking I would pick it up, like lint, on my travels, but most of the time I talked English with Lorne, or German with the *Wandervögel* we met on the highway. We did learn to count, and keep track of money, and by pointing and mugging we did all right. Italians do that naturally, and just throw in the talk to be neighborly.

The first day the wind off the mountains let up, we took off for Venice. My winter at Schloss Ranna had prepared me for what I would find in Italy, lean and hungry children, people habituated to poverty. The slap of Lorne's warped wheel on the bike fork led me to ride on up ahead a ways so I wouldn't hear it. He also had a problem keeping up with me because his old bike was so hard to pedal, and the saddle too low. It turned out that the saddle was bolted to the frame, and not on a post that he could raise or lower. Did he look forward, I asked him, to a tour of Italy on an old tricycle? That night we had a talk, and I was able to persuade him to get a front wheel that wasn't warped. He did it for me. He didn't mind the slapping noise himself.

Most of the time we had the highway to ourselves. We would pick up some food in the market, then look for a place out of the wind to eat it. Cemeteries with a wall to get behind were good, especially if the sun happened to be shining. It had always seemed to me that English poets made a point of putting off dying until they were in Italy, but after checking several hundred gravestones I had to change my opinion. One of the kids who spoke to us mentioned the name of Primo Carnera. Some of the older ones knew the names of Italian baseball players, like Tony Lazzeri. These kids would fight among themselves as to where they would take us for a night's sleep.

In a town near Venice a man and his wife got out of a bed in the front room so we could use it. The sheets were pretty soiled, so we slept in our clothes, stretched out on the top of it. The man's wife had a brother living in America. She brought in the neighbor's wife and her husband, along with several kids, to look at us. She kept repeating a word that I thought to be a person, but what she was saying was *Shik*-ago, for Chicago. That's where her brother was. Surely I must know him. Actually, I couldn't say for sure I didn't. I had come to know a lot of Italians. In the excitement of this occasion I left my wristwatch under the pillow (they unbuckle the watches while you're sleeping) and I had to pedal nine miles back for it. The signora had it strapped to her own wrist, which she explained was the safest place to keep it. One of her kids ran along beside me on the highway the way a stray dog will when you get a bit too friendly.

Approaching Venice, we met three husky *Wandervögel,* in shiny lederhosen, rucksacks on their backs, who had been to Sicily. They were on their way to Dubrovnik, wherever that was. From them we learned of student hostels in Rome and Naples, and I received my first offer for my English bike. The great thing about meeting up with Germans was to say *Auf Wiedersehen* like we meant it when we parted.

Nothing had prepared me for Venice.

It was gray and cold, the chill of winter trapped in the alleys, the people small and pinch-faced, the peddlers sly and greedy, the assorted smells (except for espresso!) nauseating, the slap-slap of the refuse-littered gray-green water smelling the way Mann had described it in *Death in Venice,* but even more than Ranna, it was out of this world, an ancient rotting city flooded by the sea. Small boys hooted and kicked soccer balls in the *campos.* At one point we were followed by an old man with small cages of chirping wild birds on his back. I sometimes wanted to leave, but we were lost, until a boy led us by the hand into the Piazza San Marco. Clouds of pigeons swirled around us, like schools of flying fish. There was surely music, but I didn't hear it. Throngs of people moved about, some of them feeding the pigeons that hovered in a blur above their heads. Bells rang. We sat at the base of a monument, facing the bay, where a white ship passed by, like a scene in a painting, and I was out of this world without a clue to which world I was in.

In a café with laborers who looked like statuary, their hands and faces white with marble dust, I saw a man crouched at the canal, water lapping his feet, rinsing in the filthy water a strip of soiled cloth that he then wrapped around his forehead, covering his swollen eye. With his good eye he studied me with indifference. A frail sallow boy, with large sad eyes, like those I had seen among the children at Ranna, led us to where we found a small clean bed, and shared our body heat. I have no memory of beauty. My jumbled impressions mingled the sordid, the earthly, and the unearthly, in a way that exceeded my understanding. We didn't talk about it. In the morning we were relieved to pick up our bikes and get away from the water. We both had new bites that began to itch when we worked up a sweat.

On clear windless days, one of them a Sunday, we crossed the Po valley from Padova to Bologna. The afternoon sun tanned our faces. Three or four times a day we met up with *Wandervögel,* and I talked more German than I had in Vienna. There was snow on the mountains between us and Florence, with strong, cold winds. Down in the valley the spring sun had warmed us, but we almost froze in the mountains. Near the summit—we saw the light, like a beacon, as we pushed our bikes up the grade —we found this smart café, with booths to sit in and a counter, rows of fluorescent lights in the ceiling, behind the counter the biggest electric Frigidaire I had ever seen. Just the summer before, it had arrived from Newark. The owner's two sons had brought it from Genoa on a truck. The owner and his beaming wife had daughters in Trenton, and had pictures of their grandchildren framed on the wall. Because we were Americans, accustomed to refrigerators, they showed us the gleaming, empty compartments. In the summer, when it was hotter, they hoped to find more use for it. The wife made us sandwiches of salami we could eat on the road. There were so many Italians in America, as I knew from personal experience, it seemed hard to account for the number that remained in Italy.

Flying down the mountains toward Florence I got so far ahead of Lorne that when I looked back for him he was gone. Nor did he show up when I stopped and waited. I had to go back up the mountain before I found him plodding along, pushing his wreck of a bike. He had blown a tire. Actually, we saw more that way, walking along together, the rocky slopes around us turning green with spring, but after a few hours of it I suggested he take off the tire and ride on the rim, since the wheel was no good in the first place. If I was in such a hurry, he said, why didn't I ride on ahead and wait for him in Florence. He rather liked walking, and if he could do without pushing a bike he might prefer it. The *Wandervögel* were free to walk, or to stop and loaf, and they were never worried about a fancy bicycle. That was a dig at me, and I answered him back, I probably hollered at him, because I knew that he was right. My bike was great to ride but it was a damn nuisance every time we stopped and I had to leave it for three or four minutes. The kids would steal the horn, the tools, the tire caps. I had to keep it right beside the bed in the room we slept in. I envied the

Wandervögel, just as Lorne did, having all their gear in a rucksack, with a bedroll on their backs.

Lorne didn't say much at all, just stood there with his flat-tired bike, gripping the handlebars with his blue hands and chapped knuckles—we both had cracked lips, windburned eyes and peeling noses—but almost all of what I said I remembered, including some comments about anybody who would come to Italy in a blue serge suit. It pretty well ruined Florence for both of us. We found a place for the night—the kids were fighting over us—just down the street from the Uffizi Gallery, but when we got up to leave in the morning the Italian wouldn't let us have our bikes. He claimed we owed him money for bike storage. He was a thick, paunchy fellow, with a bellowing voice that led people to stop in the street and stare at us. He had our bikes in the hallway, off the street, and stood in front of us blocking the door. I was all for paying him, before we got into worse trouble. As usual, Lorne said nothing. He just stepped forward and jerked the fellow's coat off his shoulders, so that it pinned his arms to his sides, then lifted him like a fat kid and signaled to me to push out our bikes, which I did. When Lorne set him down, the paunchy fellow was speechless. My big, gentle, inarticulate companion hitched his pants up a bit, the way they do it in the movies, then we walked away and left them all staring at us. We could hear the fellow shouting, but nothing happened. What it meant was that we missed seeing the Uffizi, Ghiberti's doors and Michelangelo's David, but it sure cleared the air between us. Lorne wanted to see the Leaning Tower of Pisa, so that was where we went next.

I took some snapshots of the tower, with Lorne beside it, and he took several shots of me, standing with my bike, all of which were still in the camera when we headed south for Livorno. My idea was that we would take it nice and easy, enjoying the scenery, as I had done it the year before hiking around Carmel. I had gone along with a college friend who was crazy about Robinson Jeffers, and we spent a night on the driftwood-strewn beach where we could feel the breakers pounding. I didn't sleep a wink. The beach shuddered as it did in an earth tremor. But there was nothing much to see south of Livorno, no thundering breakers, great white beaches, or sheer cliffs rising from the sea, just this big gray expanse of water and a wind that blew in our faces. You would have thought a wind coming off the Mediterranean would have been a sort of mild one, if not warm, with pauses you could blink your eyes and breathe in. This wind was so cold it made our heads and ears ache. If I opened my mouth to speak it made a hollow sound, like a bottle. To speak to each other we had to stop and turn our backs to the wind. If Italian grass along the road was greener, if the sea and the sky were bluer, if the air was softer and sweeter than it was elsewhere, we were too cold to feel it or to give a damn about it. The big trucks went by with a whoosh that sucked at us. There was no place to hide or get away from it, and if I covered my ears I could hear them buzzing.

Then I got this idea watching several of the trucks come to a halt at a railroad crossing. If we were quick, before they picked up speed, we might come up behind them and grab on to something. Why not? I had often done it in the past. It was not even easy for me to explain it, the way the wind whipped my hair. I could tell, the way Lorne licked his chapped lips, he was not so keen on it. He had a new front tire, but an old bike, and we could see that the road was full of potholes. What if we hit one at about fifty miles an hour?

I was so cold and fed up I said he could do as he pleased, but I was going to give it a try. When a big truck slowed for the tracks, I took off after it, and found a posthole I could grab. When I glanced back and saw Lorne, I never thought he would make it, with his old bike, but he hung in there with his head down, pumping like a fool, and somehow he managed. It was such a great relief to be rolling along out of the wind, the landscape streaming along beside us, we hooted and yelled like kids. On the long slow upgrades we could relax a little, but on the downgrades it was scary. We couldn't see a foot ahead. The road itself was a blur. What I hadn't figured on was that I couldn't release the grip I had on the truck and use the hand that was gripping the handlebar. Both my hands were blue with cold and numb. If I let go for a split second, and the side wind caught me, it would whip me around like a piece of paper. I had been scared before, but never with so much reason to be scared, and for so long. Lorne hung on with his head down, his teeth clenched. I finally let go near the top of a grade at what proved to be a lull in the wind. Lorne did the same a moment later, and we just let our bikes coast until they came to a stop. Our teeth chattered, and our limbs trembled. We were both too relieved to speak. I think my relief was greater, and took longer to sink in, since it had been my impulsive idea, and it shamed me to think that it might have cost my friend his life. We both knew that. We just stood there straddling our bikes, gazing out to sea. The sun was almost setting, there were breaks in the clouds, and we could see this island off the coast to the south. It looked very beautiful at that distance, and just seeing it there calmed us. The wind had let up somewhat, and we watched a farmer, on the slope below us, exercising a big dappled stallion in the farmyard. In the dusky, slanting light we could see clearly why the horse seemed so agitated. A long, black, pendulous penis, like the tongue of a wagon, wagged about beneath him. Now and then on the wind we could hear his neigh, and the thud of his hooves. One of the farmer's sons helped his father hold the rope, and the horse cantered about them in a widening circle, tossing his mane. Behind them, dramatic as a painting, the island was silhouetted against the sunset. Just as I had felt at Ranna, seeing the luminous bodies of the oxen in the dark, odorous stable, their great unblinking eyes staring at me, the scene was like a slotted window on a world that had vanished. A veil had been lifted, and for a moment I saw it just as it had been, with the gods watching, prepared to take sides if people, predictably, screwed things up.

In Grosseto we carried our bikes up three flights of stairs on the heels of a panting signora. She led us to an attic hung with drying laundry, a mattress on the floor to sleep on. The air was warm, antiseptic with the smell of strong soap. A small boy brought us plates of *al dente* spaghetti and half a liter of wine in a raffia bottle. The wine burned our tongues and our raw chapped lips.

In the morning the wind was still blowing, and we walked with our heads down, not speaking, sometimes lying out of the wind in the ditches. In the late afternoon we came out on a rise with a view of the sea. Army trucks were parked in front of a large *albergo*, where we could hear music playing. On a promontory just off the coast there were gray-walled buildings that looked like fortifications. How did the wind blow so hard, I wondered, and not stir up waves?

Though it was still daylight, we were so cold and tired we went to bed, not troubling to eat. For the first time we had a double bed long enough for Lorne to stretch out in. Food smells and the clatter of dishes came through the open transom. I thought the pounding on the door that woke me up was made by someone the following morning. I asked what they wanted, but got no answer. In his sweater and underwear, Lorne went to the door, opened out on a figure holding a lantern. By its light I could see a company of soldiers wearing hats with plumes, like Cyrano de Bergerac, and broad leather belts with swords in the scabbards. Their eyes were big in the light. Two of them were so startled by the sight of Lorne they almost toppled over backward. They all looked younger than we were, like boys in an opera, picked for how they would look in the costumes. One of them managed to remove a pistol from a holster and point it in our direction, shouting. Lorne closed the door. We listened to a great hubbub in the hall, and after a moment more pounding on the door, but not so loud. Lorne opened the door on the *albergo* proprietor. Behind him, forming a line on the stairs, we could see the plumed hats of the soldiers. In a friendly manner, with many gestures, the proprietor explained that the soldiers had come for us. Why? He rolled his eyes upward. We dressed, watched by the eyes at the door, then we were escorted down the stairs and out of the building, and put into one of the army trucks, covered with a tarpaulin. Fifteen or twenty soldiers climbed in with us, their scabbards rattling. A cold wind was still blowing off the sea, and we could see lights in the fortifications. There was no talk.

We were driven a mile or so to a railroad crossing, then along the tracks to a depot. Along with the soldiers, we were unloaded into a small waiting room. There was a wood stove at the center, but no fire. The soldiers huddled together for warmth on the benches along the wall. Those near me were beardless, too young to shave. The light of a lantern, placed on the stove, cast the shadows of their hat plumes on the walls. The zippers of my

143

jacket pockets impressed them. I could sense they were both curious and apprehensive. As time passed, a few of them slept, others cleared a space on the bench to play cards. Just before midnight, down the tracks to the north, we could hear a commotion and much shouting. Several soldiers with carbines came and stood before us. They had been awakened for this special duty, and although half asleep, tried to look determined. A few moments later a southbound express train roared through, filling the air with dust and rattling the windows. This clattering racket awakened the boys who had been sleeping, and in the silence that followed they were more relaxed.

Were we Germans? they asked.

No.

Were we then English? This seemed to exhaust their alternatives. What were we, then? I said Americans. They stared at us dumbfounded, wide-eyed, their jaws slack. We were the objects of jokes and much nervous guffawing. They took fire from each other quickly, but it did not last. I was familiar with these hoarse-voiced, dark-skinned boys who looked and sounded so much tougher than they actually were. Shortly after three o'clock a small car arrived with two men dressed as civilians, their hands thrust into the pockets of their long black coats. One of them, smiling and friendly, wore a derby.

"How it go, o-kay?" he said to me, pleased with himself.

Smiling and cheerful, like a helpful porter, he padlocked my left wrist to Lorne's right one, then put us into the rear seat of the little car. The two of us filled it, and it tilted to the side Lorne sat on.

"Bicicletta!" I cried, suddenly remembering that we had left our bikes in the *albergo* lobby.

"Is nothing!" he said, putting one hand on my arm, and gave me the wink of an accomplice. His companion wore a black hat also, but with a rim that dipped to conceal his eyes. He smoked a cigar. Bouncing along in the car, the lights flickering up ahead, it occurred to me that we were having a bizarre adventure, one of those that we would long remember. For the first time I was wearing handcuffs! "Had run-in with the *Fascisti!*" I would write on the postcards showing the Leaning Tower of Pisa. The word for this sort of thing was *lark*. We were having a lark. I had not yet read the stories of Hemingway, so I did not recognize the characters. The smaller of the two officials intrigued me. He continued to smile in a knowing, appealing manner. Something between us. I would have time to think about what it might be. Up ahead of us, the car lights played on the walls of what I recognized to be a prison.

"Where are we?" I asked.

He replied, "Grosseto."

I had never before been in an actual prison, but I had seen a lot of movies. This one was large, and impressed me. Inside the walls, inside the main structure, tier on tier of barred cells, stairways and open walkways rose toward a dark ceiling, dim as a railroad station. Our steps echoed in the silence. We all walked the length of the building to a room lit up like a lavatory. A large un-

145

shaded bulb hung on a cord from the ceiling. The man who sat at the desk, his face puffy with sleep, had just been awakened. He wore a green visor to keep the glare out of his eyes.

This glare made it hard to see the faces around us but easy to see what we took from our pockets. Our rucksacks were also emptied, the contents spread out on a large table. Our passports brought on fits of laughter. My camera was admired. With sober mockery the prison official asked me what it was I had inside it. Pictures, I replied. Of what? He ordered me to open it up so he could see them. When I refused, he opened it up himself, exposed the film to the light. He saw nothing. Did I mean to try to make a fool of him? All of the packs of film I had shot since leaving Ranna he opened and exposed in the same manner. Then he rolled each film up as he had found it, and carefully returned them to their cartons. His eyes twinkled with humor. This was a well-rehearsed joke.

When our pockets were emptied, and the contents noted, we were ordered to remove all our clothes but our socks. All three examined our bodies. We were ordered to stoop and spread our buttocks. Their pleasure in this was too intense for laughter or bantering talk. When they had looked their fill, we were given blankets and a guard marched us back down the hall. I was taken up a spiral stairway to a second tier, put into a cell with a heavy, solid door, a small trap at its center. No bars. I heard nothing through the walls. The bed was a slab that lowered from the wall on chains. What I remember is the graffiti on the brownish-green wall that I faced in the morning, the words "Il Duce" being the most recent, with appropriate illustrations. Some of the names were familiar from my years at Larrabee Y, and to them I added, with my thumbnail, my own.

Food came in through the small trap in the door, the way a baker puts loaves into an oven. With the bowl of minestrone, which I thought good, I received a wooden spoon shaped by use into a crescent. I was open to such impressions, and I was impressed. Such details were better than I had hoped for. Later that day my clothes were returned to me in a basket, but all of the pockets were empty. With my clothes back on, I began to scratch new bites.

High in the back wall a slotted open window let in a cold gray light, and occasionally I heard the wings of a bird flapping. Later, after the creaking of several doors, I stood in line with about a dozen others as we walked single file from the great hall into a small court with high walls. The armed guards on the wall did not look aggressive. First we slowly walked in a circle from left to right, then right to left, and so on. I had seen it all pictured in a Van Gogh painting, and now I could vouch for its accuracy. Nobody spoke. We were a strange and shabby lot, more like bums and hoboes than criminals. If I looked stranger to them than they did to me—and I am certain that I did—they did not let on. We could hear the scrape of other marchers in an adjoining court. At a distance I could hear the clopping of a horse, and farther still, the whistle of a locomotive. On our way back to our

147

cells we passed a group coming out, and one of them was Lorne. He blended in so well with the others, in his rumpled blue serge, I almost overlooked him. To that extent he made a better prisoner than I did, and aroused in me a pang of envy. The guard on my tier of cells, a small, elderly man, with a cap too large for his head, was the image of the one I had seen in the apéritif ads in the Paris Métro. As he pushed my food through the trap he would say, "O-kay, *sì?*" and I would reply, "O-kay."

During the day my sense of personal outrage, seldom exercised, gave way to reflections on the nature of my experience. This in turn, during the long, itchy night, gave way to a rising sense of apprehension. Who knew we were here? It might be weeks or months before anyone we knew would have reason to miss us. Under the name I had scratched on the wall I recorded my captivity.

On the third or fourth morning I was led from the cell to the office of the prison director. A heavy, bald, moon-faced man, he wore the soiled coat of his uniform unbuttoned. He looked at me, from behind his desk, with what I felt to be almost fatherly sorrow. Where had I gone wrong? We did not prove to have much of a language problem. He made faces and gestures. I made drawings on the sketch pad he had found in my rucksack. They were not good, but they were explicit. Was I then an artist? I saw that I was. What else had brought me to Italy, the home and the mother of art? Michelangelo, da Vinci, Raphael, Brunelleschi—not for nothing had I read *Art Through the Ages* and filled notebooks with reproductions mounted on three colors of paper. For him, I made a sketch of my cell, with the occupant huddled in a soiled blanket, a bird perched in the slotted window. He looked at me as Raphael's cherubs looked at the Virgin Mary. He looked, but at the time that seemed to be all. Led back to my cell, I felt that the wheels of justice might be turning but were somewhat creaky with long disuse.

The following morning actual shouts penetrated my cell. Was it a prison riot? A protest for justice? Some time later a guard came for me, and from the walkway on the second tier, I saw a stocky man standing in the lower hall, his arms crossed on his chest, like Mussolini. His clothes were well pressed, and he wore a gray, rolled-rim fedora. As I reached the ground floor, and walked toward him, he threw up his arms, cried out as if wounded, and came on the double toward me. Midway in the great hall we met and embraced, then drew back for a fresh encounter. It was clear that he knew me. His dark eyes flashed. His unshaven face was radiant with recognition. The guard escorted us to the prison office, where my new friend pounded on the desk and shouted. Lorne was brought in, and he was loaned a comb to untangle his hair. He was somewhat befuddled, but not resentful. Our belongings were returned, including our money, minus a deduction for the meals we were served. A pay-as-you-stay prison? Did it mean freedom if you ran out of money? We were both embraced by the prison director, to whom I gave the sketches, and signed them. Our benefactor, whose name still escapes me, led us out of the prison to a horse-drawn two-wheel cab, the one seat tight for the three of us. Slowly we clopped through Grosseto, dismally dreary in the drizzle, to where we were greeted and embraced by two short, substantial women. From among the many photographs on a sideboard our friend selected a snapshot, showed it to me. There I stood, both taller and paler than the dark-skinned boys on each side of me. I knew them well! Sammy and Vito LaMonica. That summer at the Y camp on Lake Hastings, both boys had come down with a bad case of ringworm. These two boys were the grandchildren of the beaming, elated man at my side. Once more we embraced. Then we were seated at the table and encouraged to eat.

Later there were more pictures, but not of me. Sammy LaMonica was married, and stood at the door of a delicatessen. Vito LaMonica drove a pie truck and could be seen in his white uniform, beside it, the plum-colored birthmark dark on his face. I was given his address on Sedgewick Street in Chicago and told to tell him to be sure to write more often. We were then driven back to the Grosseto depot, and put on a train that would stop at Orbetello. Mr. LaMonica trotted along the station platform, waving to us.

On the train to Orbetello, Lorne and I had a chance to discuss all that had recently happened, but we didn't. Not a word about the comedy at the *albergo*, or the three days and nights in prison, or how Mr. LaMonica, of all people, ever got wind of our being there. How do you figure that? I think the problem was that too much had happened, and too fast. First we had the Orbetello business, with the army like one you would see in an opera, then to top it all off, something so unlikely that Lorne didn't know what to make of it. Anywhere else he would have thought it some sort of hoax. How in the world did two Italian kids in Chicago relate to somebody like me in Grosseto? Actually, it did make sense, it was all of a piece, but I knew better than to try to explain it to a person who had just left Orange County for the first time. The Y camp that summer had been a very good one, and Vito LaMonica had had a crush on me. He had forgotten all about the purple birthmark on his face, the envy he usually had for his good-looking brother. Who else would a kid like that write to but his grandfather in Grosseto, which was what he did, telling him what a wonderful person I was. The only strange thing about the whole business was that it had worked.

We found our *biciclettas* right where we had left them, but everything that could be unscrewed had vanished, including the chains. We were so grateful to find our bikes, however, that we didn't make a fuss about it. I did make it a point to ask why, in the first place, we had been arrested. I was dying to know. The proprietor was friendly but nervous. He made the usual jokes about the Italian army being a bit confused as to who they were fighting. His wife, however, a lean, sinewy type of woman, crossed her bony arms on her flat front and assumed the posture of a monument tilted backward. There was no mistaking Il Duce. My professor friend in Trieste would have loved it. The great man himself, we learned from her, had been on the train that passed through at midnight on its way to Rome. And had I not myself been strolling around taking pictures? *Capisce?* she said.

"*Capito,*" I replied.

We could only push our bikes into the wind, or coast on them when we had a downgrade. A peasant with a wagon gave us a lift the last few miles into Civitavecchia. We got chains at a bike shop, but I found out too late, trying to pump up a grade, that the links were not right for the sprocket. The best way to enter Rome is not the way we did it, pushing one bike with a flat tire and one with a slipping chain, but with the road headed to the east, out of the face of the wind, we were able to walk along with sun in our faces or warm on our backs.

Even Lorne had heard that all roads lead to Rome, but we were so long in getting there he was sure we had taken the wrong one. We saw a lot of it trying to find the youth hostel run by the Catholics. In the Forum, green grass was growing among the ruins, and we took our shirts off and had our first sunbath. There was nobody around and we had it all to ourselves. Some of the paths were strewn with chips of marble that might have been left there by the Romans. They were all over the place, like gravel, part of a past that had not entirely vanished. I made a collection of them for my girl friend, but on reflection I put most of them back. I suspected she would think, if she didn't say, that some people were still looting Rome, like the Huns.

The padre who ran the youth hostel would have made

a great YMCA secretary. He could not only speak every language you could think of, but he could listen to them all while he was talking. He wore a dark-brown monk's robe, with a cowl, his bare feet in open leather sandals. What struck me was how clean he kept his feet. Because we were Americans he made room for us, moving out a pair of Germans he knew to be loafers. Of the sixty or so *Wandervögel* on hand, about fifty were Germans, with the rest big English fellows, or Swedes. The English fellows had been in Greece over the winter, working on a dig on one of the islands. The Swedes had been to Corfu, Crete, Cairo and all over, but nobody would ever have known it. They didn't talk, but one of them made me a good offer for my bike.

Almost everybody we met had been to Sicily, Sardinia and Capri. Actually, I didn't see as much of Rome as I might have because I liked the life and talk at the hostel. From a Swiss, at a bargain, I bought a watch with a lot of dials on the face, with levers on the side to start and stop them. They told me anything I wanted to know but the right time. Along the Appian Way, between Rome and Naples, my Swiss watch stopped running, but when I gave it a shake and held it to my ear, the ticking I heard was like Antone's, his red lips parted as he gazed, entranced, at the face without hands.

Along the coast of Italy we looked hard for something that would compare with California, but until we came out on the Bay of Naples, neither of us had seen it. A drizzle and blowing mist veiled Capri, shot through with ribbons of rainbows, and trailing off to the south, like the smoke of a steamer, the feathery plume off Vesuvius. Naples itself was something else. Since I had lived in Chicago, I was not unprepared for how things look at a distance and then you saw them close up, but Lorne had seen no more of the slummy side of life than Main Street in Los Angeles.

We started along the waterfront, then just kept rising, pushing our bikes up the alleys with gutters at the center, with flocks of kids yelling and hooting around us, as well as a nanny goat with two young ones, until we came out on a road above the city where there were gardens and walled villas. We could see Pompeii clearly, or where it had been, and several big three-masted ships in the harbor, and on the hazy horizon the isle of Capri the way it would have looked in a Maxfield Parrish painting. Not really; it was more of a purple color, like a cluster of Concord grapes. The full roll of pictures I took at the time, and had developed in Paris (I didn't see them until five weeks later), I didn't think were mine because Capri wasn't even in them. Just the jumble of roofs on the slope below us, some of the boats in the bay, and our two bikes in the foreground. Everything but the bikes was overexposed.

From the pier where we took the boat to Capri the sea was like a big pond, with hardly a ripple on it. I had thought most of the passengers would be *Wandervögel*, but they appeared to be regular tourists or Italians. The boat itself was on the small side, like a lake steamer, with a canvas to cover the open passenger section. Having sailed from New York to Antwerp, and weathered a bad storm in the mid-Atlantic, I was amused to notice how quickly some of the passengers were queasy. It surprised me, as it did Lorne, how soon the open water got rough. We all sat on hard wooden benches, around a clearing where you could walk a few paces, or stand and talk. An elderly Englishman and his tall, thin wife stood up all the way, holding on to each other.

I've forgotten how long the trip was supposed to take —it might have been an hour, or less than an hour—but after ten or fifteen minutes both men and women were leaning over the rail, so sick they were gagging, or were sprawled out on the floor with their backs against a wall. There was no letup in the pitch and roll of the boat, or anybody to help the people who seemed to need it. Lorne crouched doubled over, his head in his hands, whooping up on the floor between his knees. I had a worse problem. I was sick but I couldn't whoop up. I tried to sit so I could keep my face in the breeze, where the sea spray would cool it, but the roll was so bad I couldn't. It went on forever. There was puke everywhere. Then it calmed as quickly as it had begun, and we were inside the Capri breakwater. A few of the Italians, as well as the Englishman and his wife, walked right off. Lorne and I just sat there, unable to move, as the sicker people were helped to the pier. Others managed to walk as far as the beach and sprawl in the sand. Which was what we did. It was not a clean beach, there were dead fish on it, and it was strewn with smelly seaweed and buzzing flies. We just lay there like bodies washed up in a wreck. I remember thinking I would live on the island before I would take such a boat back to Naples. If there's a comical side to the nausea of seasickness, it's in how quickly you recover once you're on terra firma. The town of Capri was right there on the cliff above us, and by the time we got there, a pretty good climb, Lorne was ready to eat more than he had whooped up. The last of the sunset was glowing on Naples, so beautiful I could only turn away from it, and we had to make a choice from among the pack of kids shouting their offers at us. We didn't see a *Wandervogel.* They were all back in Rome, living it up.

It had been my intention, since I left California, to present myself at Axel Munthe's villa, with the view of Naples pretty much as he had described it, but once we had found it, all I did was ask Lorne to take a picture of me standing below it. I had also meant to look in on Spengler, and I hadn't, and perhaps Jakob Wassermann, and I hadn't, and it was still my intention, if the occasion offered, to look in on one or two writers in Paris, but the awe and respect in which I held these figures always led me to ask what they would see in me. I was not yet a writer. I was hardly a reader. One of my teachers at college had actually known a writer who had sent him his novel, with his name written in it, and I had felt both privileged and honored to be shown that book, and turn its pages. My interest burned with a gem-like flame, but shed little light.

We spent a week on Capri, the April weather just the way it was in California, warm in the sun but almost frosty in the shade. We saw the cliffs on the backside of the island, where the swallows were as thick as clouds of gnats, and in the early evening, from the south tip of the island, we caught glimpses of Positano and Amalfi. I planned to come back and live here, like Axel Munthe. We both figured it could be done on about forty dollars a month.

We spent our nights in a big high-ceilinged room with about twenty beds, no windows, but just the two of us were usually in it. The woman who ran it said that business picked up later. The burros that pulled the two-wheeled carts up from the beach were hardly larger than dogs, and wore hats trimmed with flowers. On the slope behind Axel Munthe's villa we would sprawl and eat the food we had bought in the market, some bread, cheese and local fruit. I had read in Munthe's book that the Italians trap and eat the birds, which was why we heard so little birdsong.

If Capri lived up to our expectations we planned to go on to Sicily, but the spring-like weather, and a bad case of hives, had got me to thinking about Paris. The only way to get rid of bites and hives was a change of clothes and a change of diet. In the *pensione* where we were staying, the favorite dish was baby octopus. When I gave the soup a stir it moved as if it were alive. My friend Lorne didn't feel about Paris as I did; he had come to Europe to see Italy, and once he had seen it he would get on a boat and sail home.

I think I might have persuaded Lorne to go to Paris with me—my record as a persuader was a good one—but

157

I wasn't sure that was what I wanted. I couldn't have asked for a nicer, more compliant companion, one who seldom took exception to my suggestions, but he was there from the time I woke up in the morning until I closed my eyes at night. He looked to me for what next. If I talked, which I did quite a bit, he moved his beret around on his head, or picked the lint off the sleeves of his coat. He was a real pal, and I would surely miss him, but some of it would be a relief. I would never meet a French girl, let alone a woman, walking around with Lorne like my bodyguard, and the only French I would speak would be to waiters and postal clerks. My girl spoke French, and sometimes put in her letters things I didn't understand.

Cycling back to Rome, we were caught in a downpour and soaked to the skin. The dye ran in the shoes I had bought in Krems and stained my feet the color of maraschino cherries. It changed my mind about cycling all over Europe. The rainy season might be ending in Italy, but it was just beginning in other places.

One of the young men I had met at the hostel in Rome was like my friend Karl in Vienna. There was something both aristocratic and military in his manner. He liked to practice his English with me, and talk about my bike. I let him ride it around a bit, to get the feel of it, and when he came up with eighty dollars American, I decided to sacrifice it. It's a relief to be free of something everybody else wants. The big thing was that without the bike I had no choice but to take the train. Lorne would feel a little less than he might have that I was running out on him. His boat sailed from Genoa, the last week in April, so he had a week or so of easy pedaling to get there, and a forty-dollar train ticket would take me up the Rhine as far as Cologne, then back to Paris. I still had, in a zippered pocket of my jacket, sixteen American Express ten-dollar traveler's checks, which would see me through the summer if I lived on about thirty-five dollars a month. I thought it a cinch. If there was one thing I had learned after seven months in Europe, it was how to live cheap —hadn't I?

The day before I left Lorne we sat up half the night talking with two Dutch boys from Amsterdam. They spoke excellent English but they were anxious to learn some American. The smaller, thinner one, who didn't talk so much, made me think of a boy I had tutored in Vienna, the way he read my lips as if to eat the words. He got so much more from language than I did it made me ashamed. They had come to Italy to be in Rome for Easter. The older boy was the first I had met to say to me there would soon be a war. When would that be, I asked him, so I could tell people, and he discussed it for several minutes with the younger one, in their own language, then he said to me, "After the Olympics," which I thought was a strange thing for him to say. That's too bad, I said, since I would miss it. We won't, said the younger one, and gave me his sweet, melancholy smile.

I was up and away early the following morning, Lorne walking with me to the railroad station, where we made plans to meet again in California, in October. I was clear to Milan, where I changed trains, before I noticed my watch was missing. In all the excitement of the night before, I had gone to sleep with it on my wrist, a sure way to lose it. I hated to lose that watch, since I had hoped to pawn it if I ran out of money in Paris, but it gave me a certain satisfaction to know the little thief who had swiped it. He could have done it earlier, but he wanted to be sure I was leaving Rome.

Seven

*I*n the Jugend Herberge, in Heidelberg, I had a room of my own with a dormer window on the park, where blond children were playing. One blond child is not unusual, but a covey of them, blue-eyed, vivacious and sturdy, their chubby legs in half socks, their pink knees scuffed, seem to be a special breed of children. After the black heads and eyes, the gaunt and sallow faces, the blue knees and bony elbows I had seen in Italy, I looked at these *Kinder* with a curious longing. That love of the blond, the Nordic, felt by Tonio Kröger for Hans Hansen and Ingeborg Holm, of the dark for the light, for the outward and the open rather than the inward and the private, was paradoxically felt by the blond themselves in their yearning for the light and sun of Greece and the enchantment of Capri.

When Hans Castorp dozed off in the snow and blizzard in the Magic Mountain, and had his dream of unearthly beauty and serenity where the blue sea lapped the sun-kissed islands, I had cried out as he did, "Lovely! Lovely!" and I was horrified, as he was, at the dream's ghastly conclusion, and that for such a vision of human bliss one must pay in blood. I understood it, but I did not accept it. In California I had experienced such moments myself, and accepted them as part of human expectations. If something whispered to me that for such expectations we must all pay dearly, I was not persuaded. I had not been tutored in seduction by Wagner, and I knew little of subconscious Faustian bargains, and at the edges of a cliff, or a yawning abyss, I simply drew back. I was not lured to grow dizzy with intoxication and jump.

Yet at the open casement window in Heidelberg, along with the keen pleasures of expectation, I registered my first presentiments that something was rotten in this picture of perfection. Behind the light and the shadow, the trilling voices of the children, lurked a danger in which we were all complicit. Was it strange that I should feel this so intensely in Heidelberg?

It was heavenly weather. On the bridge over the Neckar I stood long and long, looking at the castle, my fancy on the Rhine Maidens in the mists behind it. On the posters in the streets of Heidelberg I read that Germany, too, had a depression. The faces of the unemployed stared at me from the billboards. Most of the young I saw in the streets, however, were dressed in some sort of uniform, and seemed buoyant and assured, striding about like *Wandervögel* into the future.

In a tobacco shop, which I entered to look at some pipes, I could see someone spying on me through a curtain. In the shopwoman's smiling, unctuous manner there was something both disturbing and false. I could hear muttered whisperings behind the curtain. My sense of apprehension was unused and rudimentary, since I had felt it so seldom, but in the eyes and furtive manner of this woman I felt, and shared, a nameless disquiet. Back in the sunlight I soon forgot it.

On the Rhine boat to Cologne, American girls crowded the deck, and even those in saddle shoes looked great. It pleased me, however, not to be mistaken for one of their kind. After my winter at Schloss Ranna, in the Wachau, the castles along the Rhine seemed to me like the ruins in romantic paintings. In Cologne, where it rained all day, I saw my first movie since *King Kong,* but I forget what it was.

On the night train to Paris I again shared the compartment with several peasant women, and my own reflection in the grime-smeared window. Once more in the dawn light I saw the greening fields of France with the big two-wheeled carts, drawn by oxen, just as I had seen them the first time, and as the train pulled into the Paris station I felt I was just arriving in Europe. I had the address of a man, known to a classmate, said to be living and writing in a garret, but now that I was actually in Paris this seemed to be remarkably pointless. I walked about the streets, buying food in the markets, since I still felt intimidated by the café waiters and the way they

163

flicked their napkins at the seats of the chairs. In the Luxembourg Gardens I sagged to a bench facing the pond and the cries of the children. I was in Paris. The mauve twilight seemed to bathe me like music. Until I rose to my feet I had been unaware of the holes in my socks, and two broken blisters.

In a hotel near the Sorbonne an exception was made for the guest who would be staying for one night only. Two American girls playing Ping-Pong in the lobby woke me up. To stay clear of the one I could hear hooting, I got away from the Sorbonne, and the student crowd, and found a room behind the Cimetière Montparnasse near where the Rue de la Gaîté joined the Avenue du Maine. My room was on a turn of the stairs, where a lot of the tenants stopped to scratch matches. I had a window on the street, a chair to put my clothes on, a cot about four inches shorter than I was. The lavatory was up one flight of stairs and had the usual crouching arrangement. How do you explain the French coming up with something like that? It was not my idea of *la vie bohème,* but children crowded the street below my window, and directly across the way, a tall, handsome black man lived with a short, dumpy white woman. I often heard them fighting but it was lost on me, since they did it in French.

I had hoped to find a room for four or five dollars a week, but the landlord was not a man to dicker. He wanted his rent in advance, and counted on his fingers to make sure I understood him. A thin, dour little man, he squinted from the smoke of his dangling cigarette. His gobbler's neck stuck out of his collarless shirt like

164

those I had seen in Vienna, but he was the proud father of two enchanting little girls. They played jacks, skipped rope and shrieked like birds until they were bedded down at night. Their dark, gaunt, harrowed mother loved them so much she drove them crazy. At the door, from a window, from an upstairs room, she cried out threats, warnings and cautions. If there was a moment of silence in the street she would swoop down on them like a hawk. She dressed them like little dolls, with big bows in their hair, and seeing me at the window they would scream, *"Me voici! Me voici!"* and run about wildly.

In my boyhood I had often had the time, and the reason, to ponder the big maps on the walls of railroad stations. Maps were the canvas for my imagination. Both those that hung in railroad depots and those on the walls of schoolrooms would provide me with lifelong deceptions. What power is it that makes it possible to confuse a map with the actual, visible world?

I was living in Paris, and I had personal access to the labyrinth that spread and swirled around me, yet I would look for clues to all that escaped me in the big, maddening maps at the Métro stations. What did I hope to perceive? All that I saw was *under* the streets, not above them. As I stood there, daily pondering this puzzle, I was often suffused with the sweetly sorrowful ballads played by the musicians seated at the entrance. The wheezy, gasping accordion, the screechy violin, seemed designed to fully capture what I was feeling but escaped my observation: not the gaiety of Paris, which I found to be lacking, except in the shrill cries of the children, but the bittersweet, haunting melancholy that appealed to me profoundly. How could I explain that my buoyant optimism was so often at its ease in depressing surroundings? Before the palmy days of my years in California, *hard times* were those I understood to be normal. Indeed, what *other* times were there? Nor would I ever question that they were more real than soft times, morally superior, and the proper times for a youth to be raised in. In the spring of 1934, in Paris, I found myself in circumstances that were confining, but in times that suited my nature. Not miserable times, nor pathetic times (they, too, were there, but concealed from me), but the times that pressed from my extravagant expectations a poignant, pensive anticipation of losses. Much of this far exceeded my experience, but it spoke profoundly to my nature. Among these sentiments, if not these people, I was at home.

The city flowed with a life beyond my comprehension, but there were moments, as I stood at an intersection, or peered down a boulevard to a swirling clot of traffic, when I would experience the city as a living body, an organism like myself, cunningly pursuing its own purpose. What provoked these moments of transport? The unavoidable, palpable presence of people. They lived everywhere. That seemed to me the secret of Paris. In the shop where I bought my sour cream in the morning, hardly larger than a closet, the clatter of knives and forks, the smell of food cooking, the squalling of infants, filled the air behind the shabby curtain. A large family, they ate in shifts. A more elegant life style was surely lived elsewhere, by a lot of people, but this was one into which I intruded when I browsed, or shopped, or peered into a doorway. The city was one vast, labyrinthine dwelling, with an inhabitant in every niche of it. Voices shouted or murmured, heaps of rags blocking a doorway might be a body, involving me in the grubby life of the species. No notice was taken of me as a person. No one needed me as a person. I, too, learned to let the coins drop on the counter to reduce the counterfeits my eye was not trained for. The throng seemed and was hostile, but I was also supported by its bustling, indefatigable presence. The great sad city, in the hug of hard times, gave off its sorrow like an odorous exhalation. The seamy side of my life of great expectations found in Paris the matchless example of making do, of getting by, as a way of life. I had gotten by, to the spring of 1934, on the expedient but unexamined principle that the truly deserving would be rewarded. Surely, I was deserving. What else had brought me here, more buoyant than blighted, to this fateful season in the city of light? In every fiber of my optimism I was a deserving fool.

After all, there was nothing between me and Paris but myself. I knew nothing or nobody; nor did I know to what extent this might, or might not, be an advantage. In the presumptions of my optimism Voltaire might have found me an interesting study. I wandered about, loafed in the parks and gardens, sat gawking in cafés or reading newspapers, adding words to my unused vocabulary.

Every morning I bought sour cream, the color and

texture of butter, which I spread on a slice of whole wheat bread with my all-purpose Swiss knife. From this food I would look forward to the bowl of borscht I took at Dominique's in the evening, just off the Boulevard Raspail near the Dôme. I soon learned that the waiters were White Russians, refugees from the Revolution. They were big, jovial, imposing fellows, of the sort I had seen with the touring Cossacks. They had a flair for communications. We had a fluent and clear exchange of signs and mugging. A basket of rolls sat on the counter, into which I freely dipped my hand. I might eat four or five. My waiter, Ivan, usually put me down for two. The bowl of borscht was served with a scoop of sour cream that I would nurse through the meal like ice cream.

After this meal my feeling for Paris—a city the color of smeared newsprint, full of aging, faintly hostile people—changed from one of indignation, occasional resentment, to one of fraternal affection. Twice a week I would top it off with a café au lait at the Dôme.

Just down the street from the Dôme, on the Boulevard Raspail, was the American Club. I had discovered it by chance, seeing a young man seated in the high casement window on the street, reading. He proved to be from Waterloo, in Iowa, in the process of reading all of Balzac's novels in French. A solemn, very earnest young man, burdened with his reading and his future as a writer, he provided me with my first portrait of the artist as a young man. I liked him, but I felt his scorn for such idlers as myself. He earned a dollar a day, plus all the tea he wanted, by opening the club in the morning, serving the tea, and cleaning up after the dances. All bona fide Americans and other aliens, females preferred, were welcome at the club. The large, dark room was attractive, with the windows thrown open, and there was room for ten or twelve couples to dance to the music of a gramophone. Most of the records were battered, but the tunes were great. "Stardust" was there, sung by Bing Crosby, along with "Body and Soul" and "Ain't Misbehavin'," songs I had learned to play on the ukelele. My expertise on the gramophone was welcome, along with my selection of records. I introduced the Balboa, a California dance step the English girls found a bit confusing, but a doe-eyed, slender señorita from Madrid slipped into it like a stocking. There was no learning. She raised her arms and we danced. She favored wide-brimmed hats, long flowing scarves, and cloth gloves with a silken, flesh-like texture. When we were better acquainted she would take them off when we held hands at the movies. French being the language we had in common, we both gave it considerable attention. No language is so marvelous to hear from the lips of a girl. Her idol was the dancer Argentina, with whom she had studied, but the shadow I often saw in her eyes was her coming marriage, in the late fall, to a businessman in Buenos Aires. She showed me his picture. He was a nice-looking gray-haired old man, at least fifty. I was not a prospective suitor, but this blighted our hours together.

An English girl from Surrey, hair bobbed, neck shaved, erect, perky, stiff as a board and plainspoken, danced with me in the manner of a sturdy colleague supporting a weaker friend. The space between us we filled with conversation. She did not like to sit, and did most of her talking with her arms folded, while standing. She thought the French politically anemic and as we walked around Paris, we discussed what it would lead to. Her own life was pretty well settled, since she planned to breed and raise fox hounds in Surrey.

If I walked her to her pension, near the Étoile, it might be past midnight before we got there, and I would spend the rest of the night slowly making my way back to Montparnasse. Nothing could be more enchanting than Paris at dawn: absolutely silent, the light in the sky part of an awakening that came by inches, the Eiffel Tower the hub around which it wheeled, the street lamps perceptibly cooling to globes without shadows. The last mile or so I might be so tired I would sit on a bench at the Gare Montparnasse until the first café clattered open, then blow myself to a café noir and a croissant. By sleeping right through until about four o'clock, I saved more money than it had cost me.

Two blond sisters from Holland sometimes came to the club for the dances. One was on the plump side, but very good-looking. She usually referred to her sister as "fatty." This was just one of many things that made her laugh. When she first set eyes on me, she laughed, and looked around for something to sit down on. Once something started her off, as I seemed to, she couldn't stop. Her big, broad face was usually flushed and perspiring, her frizzly hair stuffed into a hairnet. When she was seated on a bench, her feet were inches short of the walk. I would usually give her a hand to hoist her, and this would set off a fit of laughter. Everything we saw was either mildly funny or hilarious, and if we went to a movie at the Cinéma Montparnasse we might have to leave to avoid a disturbance. Once started, it always ended up with her chewing on her hairnet, her eyes full of tears.

We got along so well together I thought of renting the room on the floor above me, with a double bed and a carpet, but she couldn't bear the idea of my seeing her without her corset. Details of that sort had not crossed my mind. Once it had crossed, and recrossed, several times, it was hard to dislodge. When the humor of it had finally dissipated there was nothing much between us but a bulging figure dimly seen through a screen of curtains. It wasn't funny at all. Perhaps she learned from me that no matter how she looked, it was something she should let a boy judge for himself, especially if he was Dutch.

Tea was poured at the club by Madame Champfleur, a handsome, formidable woman, who preferred to sit back in the room's shadows, as if the light from the windows might fade her. She wore black, except for two long strands of pearls. A wide-brimmed crownless hat, worn low on her forehead, allowed only occasional glimpses of her eyes in the powdered mask of her face. Large bruises of rouge stained her cheeks. Rather than the wide mouth of most Parisian women, painted over the pleats of their lips, Madame Champfleur had no more than a slit through which she sipped her tea. Her voice was husky. Cigarettes had given her a throaty

171

cough. Two or three minutes of real French conversation could be bought with an offer of an American cigarette. She had known Rodin, and could speak personally of his scandalous behavior with his models. To catch the glance of her eyes, as I sometimes did, through the shafts of light from the windows gave me the ponderable sensation of being seen and judged by a woman, rather than being looked at by a girl. Both her chin and her nose were those of an admiral, but my untrained imagination often applied itself to the miracle of her morning toilette. Each day a face to be painted, then the long teetering walk, her cloak held close to her body, as if the eyes of the world were upon her, enduring the gauntlet of the sidewalk cafés to the corner of Montparnasse and Raspail. There, if held by the light, she would pivot slowly to gaze about her at the *canaille*.

I twice visited her apartment, a room her sister would depart on my arrival so there would be a chair for me to sit on. A mistake. My sympathy for the underdog did not include a woman whose grand illusions were what I admired, and was eager to support. The air reeked of soiled garments, cheap perfume, and canned food heated on hot plates. It shamed me to share this with her. I did learn that her remarkable and singular appearance was of Scottish origin, and when she referred to dastardly events of the past she had in mind the Huguenot wars. Intricate and cunning passages of French culture had made her, to my mind, one of its ornaments.

Before I had ever looked on the ground glass of a camera, the windows of Vienna and Paris had framed views that seemed part of my life, before they were part of my experience. They alerted me to the needs of my nature. People about whom I knew nothing, who were strangers to me, like the marching figures in the *blind Garten,* prefigured what I would look for and find corroborated in what I would come to imagine.

In the street below there is the following group: a small, double wheelbarrow pushed by a woman; lengthwise across the front of it, a hand-organ; across it at the back, a basket in which a quiet young child is standing on firm legs, happy beneath its cap, not wanting to be made to sit. From time to time the woman turns the handle of the organ. Then the child immediately gets up again, stamping in its basket, while a little girl in a green Sunday dress dances and beats a tambourine uplifted towards the windows.

I did not read this passage from Rilke's *The Notebooks of Malte Laurids Brigge* until ten years later. How could another pair of eyes see so clearly what I saw at the back of my own? In the old world I perceived, through the veil of my expectations, realities that predated American experience, but this did not explain my growing preference for the losses. The child happy in its cap, the girl in her Sunday dress, a tambourine uplifted toward the windows.

Twice a week I would take the long walk from the Boulevard Montparnasse to the Avenue de l'Opéra, and ask for my mail at American Express. I usually crossed the Pont Neuf, fronting Notre Dame, loafed my way through the Tuileries, then savored the *haute monde* of the shops along the avenue. My girl was a good writer of letters. They were seldom less than three or four pages, and sometimes thickened to ten or twelve, written on both sides, and not always numbered. Her very personal "hand," a horizontal line like that of ripples on the surface of water, with an occasional loop or splatter, had the fluency of her voice and style, but the gist of the matter escaped me. What *was* she saying? Having the time, and the interest, I gave it much thought.

She was majoring in French, and full of her subject. Did she, when she mentioned Versailles, urge me to go there or not to bother? To be sure and read Saint-Simon, or forget him? I was not a good tourist. I had only twice been to the Louvre. Mona Lisa's enigmatic smile put me very much in mind of Mizi, with her oval eyes and pale, suds-laced arms. In my own, briefer letters I had touched on a new book, recently published, *Les Célibataires*, by Henri de Montherlant. I hadn't bought it, but somehow I had read it. This story of two old men involved me in a way that many stories of young men failed to. In the constrained, monotonous pattern of their lives—which I perceived and sensed in the streets around me—I shared a truth about people, and my own nature, that transcended differences of culture. This painfully obvious observation, in applying to me, personally, seemed a fresh one. My father, my relations, the few older men who had figured, briefly, in my transient life, had left on me impressions that I had hardly been aware of. Was this peculiar to France, to the French language, to the book I happened to be reading? I was aware that a writer had

174

revealed to me much I had overlooked within myself. How was that done? My impressions were blurred, but my inadequate French may have enhanced the images of my imagination. I carried Montherlant's novel about with me. I read certain passages over and over. In the complex craft of writing I sensed that the art of it combined what was new with what was old. What was new would prove to be in the writer, and the writing.

At the club I heard the name of Céline mentioned as the author of *Voyage au bout de la nuit.* I was captivated by the haunting title. I also understood that much of it was in an argot impenetrable to foreigners. There were other appealing inducements.

On the Right Bank, on a street of bookstores, I found a mint copy of the novel on one of the tables at the front. The price was the cost of four or five days in Paris. I hovered about the table in a quandary. The uncut pages of the book inflamed my desire for it. Stealthily, with what little cunning I had, I slipped the book into my unbuttoned shirtfront. Before I could button up, before I had moved from the spot, a figure swooped from the interior of the shop to seize me, expertly, by the collar and the seat of my pants—as I had so often seen it done in the comics—and projected me, hardly touching the floor, through the shop to an office at the back.

So I had made a mistake.

My twisted arm held firmly at my back, the proprietor emptied my pockets, then put through a call to the police. A short, bullheaded man, his sleeves rolled on pow-

175

erful arms, a film of perspiration on his fleshy face, he barked questions at me I did not understand. My money was on the table, but what he wanted was the thief. The pleasure that it gave him to catch me competed with his hatred for me. He panted with his excitement when he found and flicked through my passport. An *Américain!* That pleased him. The two gendarmes who appeared also searched me, and my trousers were lowered to look for books in my crotch. They then walked me, my shoulders hoisted to my ears, along the crowded boulevard to an alley, up narrow stairs to an office. A little fellow with bright, darting eyes sat behind a large desk. He spoke sharply to the gendarmes, and they left. Courteously, with a smile, he asked me to be seated. We considered each other—or rather he considered me, his face veiled by the smoke of his cigarette. He seemed amused and delighted. Not every day did they bring him one like me. I remembered the plainclothes pair in Orbetello, who had also been elated by their unusual catch. So what was it I had stolen? A book. And what was the book? I told him. If I had confessed my love for France, for law and order, for the police, I could not have delighted him more. He gazed at me with appreciation. The edge of his scrutiny sharpened. Was I then a student of literature? I was. He paused to offer me a Gauloise, and light it. We smoked for a moment in silence. Did I then—he asked me—plan to be a writer? Oh fateful question! Did I? Had I waited to be asked? Montherlant's novel had aroused in me not merely the heightened pleasure of reading, of self-recognition, but the latent stirrings to be writing, to

176

be that curious conjuror, a writer. Did he perceive in my flushed, perspiring face the lineaments of this recognition?

Briefly, we discussed books. I mentioned Gide and Henri de Montherlant. He made note of *Les Célibataires* on his pad. He then brusquely dropped his role as a man of letters and examined my passport, asked my residence, and inquired into my financial situation, facts I had been keeping from myself. He jotted this information into a ledger while I gazed at the sky through his window. It had begun to drizzle. I did not like rain, but the Paris drizzle seemed to me the most appropriate of its moods. I thought it gave a touch of welcome pathos to my foolish predicament.

He advised me to report back to him, within a month, with evidence that I was self-supporting. Some things that he said I did not understand, but I was reluctant to admit it. I very much appreciated his admiration. But now that he saw me for what I was, for what *we* thought I was, he also lost interest. Another culprit was brought in, with a bruised and bloody face, and I was led to the foot of the alley, and left there. I could have hooted with relief when I walked in the street. The book I had failed to swipe would have instructed me in the risks that are run in small offenses, and in the days left to me in Paris I spent a lot of time glancing behind me. I was on *parole*, one of the words I had clearly understood.

A young man I might have spoken to but had avoided was an English chap from Tangiers. He was about my age, but more experienced. Not one of the big, handsome fellows, pillars of empire, but a short one with a savoir faire I admired. He courted several women. He dressed very smartly in tweeds and sweaters. He played a lot of Ping-Pong with some of his friends, but I was the one he was anxious to beat. He got one of his flunkies to proposition me with a deal I couldn't turn down. He gave me odds of five to one on every point. My big mistake was in settling for a franc a point. If I had had his nerve I would have made forty or fifty francs every time we played. He wasn't a really good player, but he took all the chances, as if he didn't give a damn about winning or losing. Two or three of his flunkies ran around chasing the balls he slammed. We both soon tired of playing Ping-Pong, and spent the evenings in his apartment listening to records. He had American jazz, American novels, and three or four bottles of American whiskey he served with seltzer from a siphon bottle. We had some long, frank talks, especially about women, and what he liked about me was that I was a loner. I didn't live with a woman, mix with a group or run around licking asses. That was what he said. If that was what it was to be a loner, I qualified. Most of his flunky friends were not loners, but a pretty sad bunch of hangers-on, who thought driving around in a Packard with its top down, the horn honking, was really hot stuff. They did a lot of that on Saturday and Sunday nights. Sometimes we all went for a ride out to the Bois de Boulogne, where we played catch with an indoor ball, and batted flies. They really weren't obnoxious, individually, but they acted like fools when they got together. My Tangiers friend said that I should put all of us into a book.

He didn't brag, to speak of. He would just let it drop that he had been on safari. One thing he did tell me about at length was the time he had come down, in the bush, with dysentery. Unable to go to the bathroom, like a normal person, he had to put long hairs in the food he ate so it could be pulled out of him, if necessary. I had never heard of anything like that, nor had he.

One evening my friend, seated back under the awning, yahooed at me as I was passing the Dôme. He was there with two girls, both of them good-looking, one of them the blond sister of my laughing Dutch girl. She was one of those big, handsome types who like to wear a fur piece in the summer. The other one was German, with a dark, creamy complexion, like Mizi. When I arrived they were in a big discussion about the coming war. Both girls believed it would be better if the French didn't fight the Germans, as they did the first time, but just let them run the government since they seemed to be so good at it. Why blow up everything, and kill so many people, if all they wanted to do was have parades and play big shots? My English friend said that it would never work because men loved war, and down deep, women loved warriors. I was startled to be part of such a crazy discussion over something they expected to happen. In their excited, animated faces, I sensed that anything would prove to be acceptable if we knew it would end up as talk. Talk was what it was all about.

When we had the war settled, my friend led me to the

men's room, where he groomed his hair with small hairbrushes he carried in his pocket. What he wanted to do was ask me a little favor. You name it, said I. He happened to have a little conflict in his appointments, and found himself with these two great dolls in one evening. Would I be good enough to take the blonde off his hands? He could see, he said, that she had high respect for my kind of brains. He peeled off several bills from the wad in his pocket, and mentioned the sort of places where she liked to eat. I said I would do him the favor. We came back to the table, where we sat for twenty minutes while the girls went below and tidied up. I couldn't see this blonde, who had ignored me for months, agreeing to take a back seat to this classy brunette, but she seemed to welcome the change. My friend also threw in a pack of Player's cigarettes, since that was what she smoked.

I didn't want to start off blowing money on a taxi, so we strolled down Montparnasse, through the Luxembourg Gardens, then out onto the Boul Mich and the Boulevard St. Germain. We stopped for an apéritif at the Deux Magots, where a different sort of crowd was passing, and after a bit of the usual chitchat she asked me what it was I was writing. I said I was doing more reading than writing, but that I did make a few notes. My friend had let it drop that I was an American writer with connections with the *Atlantic* and some other magazines. She knew a painter or two back in Holland, but she didn't know many American writers. We had another apéritif and she confessed that she had missed the real bohemian side of Paris because her friend always took her to the fancy restaurants. She saw that as a difference between Americans and Englishmen.

At one point I thought we might go to Dominique's, where I had heard violins playing in the basement, but on second thought, liking a change myself, I took her to a café near the Pont Neuf, with a view of Notre Dame. When she excused herself to go to the ladies' room, to be on the safe side I checked to see how much money he had given me. Almost four hundred francs. A big Dutch girl, not as yet corrupted by the idea of a light, nonfat diet, she was still at it late in the evening, one of her real passions being the cheese tray. Early on, the wine had loosened my tongue, and I revealed my life in a Fascist prison. She urged me, she beseeched me—between the distractions of the cheese tray—to write a book. On a piece of paper torn from her list of phone numbers she wrote her name and address in Holland, where I would send the volume the moment it was published. We had been sitting so long it was her idea that we should walk. Her pension was on the Right Bank, near the Étoile, and the summer night was balmy. We crossed the Pont Neuf to the Île de la Cité and headed west, along the river. Although she seemed very different than her sister, and need not worry so much how she looked in a corset, a little wine and a lot of cheese had brought out much that we had in common. She liked to laugh, but she could do it without collapsing. Where there were benches we might sit down while she rested her feet.

We had been walking for quite some time when I was

struck by something peculiar. The bench we were on, and the view of the river, as well as what I could see, glancing around me, looked almost identical to where we had been when we started. And so it proved to be. I had forgotten we were on the Île de la Cité, and that following the wall we had walked around it, maybe several times. She had kicked off her shoes to rest her feet, but when she learned what had happened she keeled over with laughter. So did I. We had to lean on the stone wall for support. It then proved impossible to get her shoes back on her swollen feet. In her stocking feet, she leaned on me for support, and we made our way back to the Pont Neuf, where we had started. I managed to flag down a taxi. He was one of those mousy little pop-eyed fellows like the apéritif ads in the Métro, but for all his experience, he said, we had given him something new to consider. I set him up with a big tip. It was something special the way she ran her hands through my hair.

I was so pooped I could hardly stand, but I also had this habit of walking at night, so I didn't take a taxi. On one of the benches along the Seine I fell asleep. For one reason or another the gendarmes didn't find me, and I treated myself to fried eggs, the way the French do them, at the Dôme. What sort of night had my friend had with his brunette? When I saw him he called me "old buddy," and didn't bring up the problem of money. After the whole business I still had almost two hundred francs.

Why didn't I take some of this money and blow it on one of the girls I had seen at the Dôme? I had observed them for weeks. One of them, with slick black bobbed hair, her eyes like Kiki of Montparnasse, stored her gum behind her ear when a customer approached her table. This left a spot white as a Band-Aid. She had once turned her eyes on me, seen nothing of interest, turned away. Sometimes I sat so close to her table I saw the smoked butts stored in her cigarette case. In one of my fantasies I would approach her table, smile and offer her one of my Camels. She had her own lighter. I could hear its click, several tables away, like the key of a typewriter. My scenario provided several witty openings, and went as far as her door, off the Rue de la Gaite, where I had seen her disappear with more confident lovers. The siren song "How could anything that felt so good be all that bad" had been sung to me, and I had listened, but the specter of disease kept me in line. My YMCA experience had been long and explicit, with lectures, sermons and pictures, including an unforgettable visit to the venereal ward of a Chicago hospital. I hesitated to use or pronounce such words as *syphilis* and *gonorrhea.* With the word *clap* I was familiar, and on speaking terms. But if I should catch the clap, what would I do? There were streets in Paris, and open doorways, where the smell of ether led me to seal my lips, and my glimpse into waiting rooms confirmed my worst suspicions. Whatever hell might be elsewhere, this struck me as hell on earth. If these facts slipped my mind for a moment, I also had my girl to think of. On those long walks through the streets at night I would sing to myself "Ain't misbehavin', I'm savin' my love for you," a pact I shared with many of my generation. More than what I had been taught, or read, or pondered, the songs of my adolescence evoked emotions that established profound priorities. It might be regrettable, it was often foolish and pathetic, but that was how it was for Gatsby, and that spring in Paris how it was for me. No misbehavin' to speak of. The Dutch girl had laughed herself out of my reach.

I was seated at the Coupole, having a cognac, reading the headlines of the *Paris-Soir* held by the young man at a table near me. A tall, good-looking fellow, with a clipped mustache, he had draped his summer jacket over the back of his chair and turned the sleeves of his shirt back on his tanned forearms. A packet of Player's cigarettes was beside his lighter, and he had collected four or five saucers under his glass of black coffee.

"You like this paper, matey," he said, "I'm done with it."

I didn't want his paper, but I accepted one of his cigarettes. "Rolled for me by hand," he said, "in the Virgin Islands," which was the first time I had heard that. He flicked his lighter and lit it for me. Back home in Cambridge he mostly smoked a pipe, but when he took his holiday he shifted over to cigarettes. Could I explain that? I said that I had personally found that cigarettes were easier to carry, the pipe requiring the pipe, the pouch and the pocket to be stored in. He looked dumbfounded. "You bloody bugger!" he said. "I think you've got it! It's not just one pipe you need, it's half a dozen. Then there's the bloody matches. You can't light a pipe proper, you know, with a lighter. Ruins the tobacco.

What you get in the draw is the bloody fuel!" He took his jacket from the chair and slipped it on the way a lot of girls do, as if his arms were double-jointed. "I've got to run, matey. Why don't I see you tomorrow? This is my table. If you like cheese, try the Welsh rabbit. Very good here, but you've got to like cheese. The frogs are clever when it comes to food." He put his pack of Player's cigarettes on my table and hurried off to flag down a taxi. He waved from the cab. I had never met a fellow just like him before, or heard the French referred to as *frogs.* He had also left a big tip on the table, which the waiter pocketed, rolling his eyes.

Since I didn't have anything very pressing to do I was back under the awning the following evening. The waiter, Louis, seemed pleased to see me. I let him bring me the Welsh rabbit, and a glass of white wine.

My friend arrived so late I first thought he had set me up. He didn't comment on it, just ordered some cognacs, and we sat smoking from his tin of Balkan Sobranies. His name was Harrow. He was married, with three children. He showed me the snapshots of two tall boys, a small girl and a short, long-faced woman. Every year, if he could manage, he took a holiday in Paris. He was a good talker, but like most Britishers he could be heard by the people at the tables around us. He liked to pump his sleeves up and down his arms as he talked. He wanted to know all about me, and I told him. What he envied me was my freedom. With whom was I living? Right at the moment, I said, I was solo. He thought that showed brains, since in his opinion women were expensive and a bloody nuisance. He took an apartment for a month every summer, but he never occupied it for more than three weeks. Would I like to have it for a week, just for a change? It was new and modern, with plenty of hot water. He simply couldn't get enough of a good hot tub himself, and soaked every day.

I said I didn't feel the need to change my apartment now that my stay in Paris was ending, but if the truth were known, I hadn't soaked in a tub, really soaked, that is, since I had left California. Great! he cried. How about this evening? At that moment I couldn't think why not. "While you soak I'll mix the drinks," he said, and walked me up Montparnasse, passing the Dôme, where quite a few people seemed to know him.

He lived in one of the modern apartment buildings on the Boulevard Raspail. Harrow's place was very smartly furnished but it seemed small once the two of us were in it. The bed was one of those that fold against the wall when not in use. The tub was built into the wall of his bathroom, with a place at the end where a person could sit. He sat there as the tub filled with hot water. "You can soak as long as you like, matey," he said, and gave me one of his wooden hangers for my clothes. I was long accustomed, at the Y, to dressing and undressing in front of strangers, but in the confines of the bathroom I was ill at ease. There were holes in my socks, and my shorts were soiled.

"You've got great legs, matey," he said to me. "You know that?" They were good straight legs, and could run, but I had always thought them too much on the lean side. In the mirror on the door I could still see where my California tan began and ended. "You like it hot or just normal?" he said. "Just normal," I replied, but when I stepped into the tub it made me gasp. "I'm a good scrubber, matey—how about me scrubbing your back?" He worked up a good lather with the soap, and gave me a scrubbing with a stiff brush. "Sorry about that tan," he said, and slowly massaged the muscles of my neck and shoulders. "How's that feel?" It felt wonderful. I had never experienced anything like it. "You've got the skin of a baby, matey, did you know that?" No, I hadn't known that either. "Sit up," he ordered, and I sat up so he could dip his hands to the small of my back. Suds floated on the water before me like icebergs. I was so relaxed I felt disembodied. A vaporous cloud of steam fogged the doorway, where Harrow stood gazing at me. I sprawled there, floating, till the water had cooled, and I almost dozed off. Music was playing, and I listened. I was surprised to see Harrow, in his pajama bottoms, at the door with a bottle and a large brandy snifter. He poured a little of the brandy into the snifter. "They say they make it out of apples, matey. Take a sniff of it." The scent of apples made me think of Schloss Ranna. What would the Meister think of my Paris adventure, floating in a tub of hot water?

A towel around my waist, I stepped out of the bathroom, to see that the bed had been lowered from the wall, and Harrow was in it. He raised his glass to me, but my sip of the brandy burned my tongue and filmed my eyes. "I like Paris in August," he said. "Fewer people.

187

The frogs leave the town, as you probably noticed."
Actually, I hadn't noticed anything so obvious. He patted
the bed at his side. "Make yourself at home, matey.
Room service in the morning. No need for you to get up
until you feel like it."

He turned from me to switch off the light, tap a cigarette from the pack, light it. By its glow when he inhaled
I could see the narrow gold band on his third finger. In
the street below the window, cars were passing. Farther
away, on Montparnasse, I could hear horns tooting. Did
I have a fever? My body felt hot between the cool sheets.
Harrow turned on his side, and in the pause of his
breathing I felt the weight of his hand on my thigh. My
heart pounded in my throat. My lips and mouth were dry.
Harrow raised on his elbow to ask, "You feel okay,
matey?" I was unable to speak. "It's the brandy," he said.
"You're not used to it. When you add the brandy to a
soak in the tub . . . You think you'd like a little fresh air?"

Yes, I thought so. In the dark, seated on the bed, I
groped for my shoes. In them I found a pair of his own
clean socks, and I pulled them on. Getting into my shirt
was not easy, with the film of sweat on my arms and
shoulders. As I opened the door he called out, "Don't
forget the address, matey. Just push the buzzer."

The perspiration on my body cooled as I walked. On
Montparnasse most of the tables and chairs were pushed
back under the awnings; a few waiters were hosing down
the sidewalks. My steps echoed in the silence. Twice I
heard and felt the rumble of the subway, like a sleeper
muttering in his sleep. My relief was so great I was buoy-

ant and elated, but it soon passed. Harrow had treated me kindly, and with respect, and I could not honestly say he had deceived me. If there had been any deception, I had deceived myself. The relief I felt to have escaped what I feared cooled to a shamefaced embarrassment. Harrow, too, had had his expectations. Had I led him on?

Two or three days later, as I was passing the Dôme, he stood up to call to me and beckon me to his table. "You had me worried, matey. You know that? You had palpitations. My fault for dosing you with the brandy. Here," he said, giving me one of his cards. "When you come to England be sure to look me up."

"Look me up," I replied, "when you come to California," but I was relieved not to have an address I could give him. As I walked away, feeling his eyes on my back, I sensed that I had overstayed the impulses that had brought me to Europe. My role as an innocent was over. I was now in the shoes of a prodigal son.

My Tangiers friend and his buddies took me with them to a taxi dance near the Bastille. Were my impressions unreal, or surreal? The dance floor had a low wooden fence around it, with gates that opened when a bell clanged. Toughs in tight caps and turtleneck sweaters, the girls with frizzly hair and painted faces, met at the center of the floor and without a word began to dance. When the bell clanged they would uncouple and leave the floor. Nothing was said; you just gave the girl a deadpan stare, and she gave you one. I hopped around in a sort of polka with a girl who never once glanced at my face. A lot of elevator dancing among the regulars (no steps), the man slipping his hands inside the girl's coat, low down on her back, coupled like a pair of stalled wrestlers. We all ended up with a lot of unused dance tickets. How would they behave, I wondered, if they didn't have the bell to break up their smooching? My Tangiers friend warned me, whatever I did, not to slip and make a pass at one of the girls, as if he thought I might.

I was watching a collection of street acrobats, the men in their soiled underwear, lift weights, bend bars and break a few chains while a kid in a clown suit beat on a drum. It took about twenty minutes. When it was over my pockets had been picked.

I don't know how he did it, but he got my billfold, with about twelve dollars in francs and the address of the mystery woman in Mallorca, my ace in the hole. What I had left in traveler's checks was ten dollars less than my freighter passage. I was too depressed to do much more than lie in my room. On the landing above me, in a room like mine, lived a paunchy, balding, middle-aged man who ran some sort of dirty-postcard racket. He was from New Brunswick, New Jersey. Why a man of his age would come to Paris I didn't understand. Now and then I saw him with one of his floozies, but I was careful not to act too friendly. He had once asked me what I did for money, and I had let it drop that I was a writer. He didn't read anything, so far as I could tell, but he had a lot of respect for writers. In one way or another he noticed that I was holed up in my room.

I let him knock two or three times before I let him in. It was one of those godawful, muggy summer nights that most Parisians leave town to get away from. He took the chair at the window, his plump, sallow face glistening with sweat. I wasn't sick, but he could see I was sick at heart. I told him what had happened, but fibbed a bit about the money I had had in the billfold. He offered to lend me five dollars, which I much appreciated but declined. Did I know, he said, that if an American citizen went broke in Paris the consul would ship him home on an American boat? No, I didn't know that. It revived me on the spot. Did he know what he was talking about? He swore that he did. The proof he offered was that the one person who had tried it, known to him personally, was not seen in Paris again. The thing you had to really be, of course, was broke. I could manage that easily enough by just spending the money I had kept for my passage. I could also have checked up on his story by going to the embassy, on the Place de la Concorde, which I had often gazed at with mixed emotions. Why didn't I inquire? I didn't want to hear what I might be told. To leave Paris at that moment, in a depression, and arrive in New York early in August, would pretty well take the bloom off the whole year and leave me stranded in New York. I wasn't expected in Cleveland, where my girl lived, until the first week of September.

On the strength of that hearsay I cashed my checks, all

191

fifty dollars of them, and watched my candle burn at both ends. Back in May I had hinted to my girl that if her Ivy League brother had an extra sweater I just might find a good use for it. In August I was notified that it had arrived. To get it I rode the Métro across Paris into the dismal, dreary torpor of the slums. I had not read Céline, but this day's long journey would prepare me for that experience. I lost my way, wandered about in the heat, and finally faced a clerk so consumed with rage at life in general that his lips frothed white as he talked. His rage was not at me, luckily, but at *them*. Even while speaking to me he would turn away to shake his tight fist at *them*. I thought surely he would take his revenge on me—the only person handy, one who had just been sent an elegant, combed-wool sweater—but his hatred of the system was so great that he took my side, and ignored the duty charges. When I thanked him he embraced me, his two-day beard rough on my cheek.

I put off to the last my visit to the U.S. embassy. A long and broad flight of marble stairs led me up to the consul's office. He was a good-looking man, sweating in his suit coat, like the one from Boston I had met in Vienna, a decent, stuffy sort of cultivated man. As I told him my story about the picked pocket, he sat polishing his pince-nez glasses. One of the many things I had picked up in France was what *pince-nez* meant, and that pleased me. Are the true stories the ones that often sound so false? I should have gone to the police, he said, not to him— it gave me a start to hear him say that—and he advised

192

me to be more careful in the future. Did I read the papers? Had it come to my attention that there was a depression in America? It had come to my attention, and it was on my mind, I said, since I did not have the money for my return passage. Had he heard what I had said? He had heard it so often he felt neither indignation nor amusement. Picking at his sleeve, he asked me why I had brought this very personal matter to his attention. I should write to my family, my friends, or even my enemies if they had any money. The American embassy was not a travel bureau or a charitable organization. Many steamers might be filled with penniless Americans who would return to the States if their passages were free.

We sat in silence. He saw through me so well that I was able to see, with humiliating clarity, just the sort of young panhandler I was.

"What am I to do?" I asked him.

This sober query startled both of us. It had just popped out. He interleaved his fingers for a moment, then said that he could get me, he thought, a second-class passage on an American steamer, but I would be obliged to repay it. I knew about how much such a passage would be, and how unlikely it was that I would be able to pay it back. In this state of depression I left his office, and started down the stairs. I made a better impression when I was not acting. From the top of the stairs his secretary called to me. It embarrassed the consul to say so, but he crisply advised me that if all else failed, he might get me a little money. How little might it be? I said my freighter fare was about sixty dollars, a sum of money small enough to impress him. If I would come back in a few days he would let me know.

During that period of waiting I was offered a job in the porn book racket (my job to paste the illustrations in the paperback books), watched the puppet shows in the Luxembourg Gardens, and made the acquaintance of a man with a pet penguin that toddled along beside him on a leash. When the bird got dirty from the gravel paths the man would dip him in the pond and wash him off. The little fellow liked that, honking excitedly like a baby duck. That was one of the things I hoped to tell people later, but when the time came I seldom did. I'm not even sure that my girl really believed it, but she felt I was entitled to one yarn like that, if it made me happy.

When I had the nerve to go back to the consul, he had gone on his vacation, but he had left a check with his secretary. She felt obliged to tell me, speaking frankly, that in actually giving me money he had departed from a department policy of long standing, and still felt of two minds about it. What sort of an example to American youth was I, she asked me, and left me at the top of the stairs to think about it.

How do I explain that all the mirrors and windows of Paris had not returned to me one remembered reflection. What did this young American really look like? He *had* lost weight: the gabardine suit he couldn't get into at Schloss Ranna hung slack on him, and the cuffs were frayed. He still retained the moustache, but who in Paris had cut his hair? On the credit side, my friend the willowy Spanish dancer, on the subway on our way back from the Bois de Boulogne, placed her gloved hand on my tanned one and confided that I was a person of good character.

This comment both pleased and puzzled me, since I had for so long taken it for granted. What reason did I have for such self-esteem?

In the last week of August I took the night train to Antwerp, where I waited for two days for the freighter to New York. I shared a cabin on the *Black Tern* with at least two others, but I have forgotten their names and faces. Most of the time I sprawled in one of the lifeboats, trying to get a tan.

I had anticipated wondering what it would be like to really understand what people were saying around me, but it wasn't much. What I remember is the long row of washbasins in the lavatory of the YMCA, and the toothbrush I bought, with the bent handle and the really stiff bristles. I sometimes felt I hadn't really brushed my teeth since I had left. At a stand on Forty-second Street, from where I could read the news going around the Times Building, I had a Coke without enough crushed ice, then took the night bus for Cleveland, sitting where the breeze off the river blew cool in my face.

Once upon a time—and a very good time it had been —I had begun an adventure that was now over. A time that I had thought I had put far behind me now loomed up around me, at the fringe of the bus lights, where the telephone poles emerged out of the darkness, the wires rising and dipping, rising and dipping, as I had once seen them from a train's diner windows.

I had a seat close behind the driver, watching the insects splatter on the windshield. Back from the winding highway, veiled by the trees, lights glowed at curtained windows, and up ahead, hooded by the night, arcs of light hung over empty corners. I was full of the mystery of the time that had passed, the *Wanderjahr* that was already far behind me, and the time that I could now hear within me, like a clock that had just started. On several occasions at Schloss Ranna I had seemed to see through a crack in the veil of one time into another, but what I had seen through were the cracks in my extravagant expectations. Had I put all that behind me? Or was I doomed to see it wherever I looked, up ahead where the dark fields of the republic rolled on under the night.

A swarming hive of insects blurred the streetlights, pinging at the screens of windows and doorways, and as these lights blinked and receded, the ticking of the clock within me grew louder. Through no fault of my own, the time that had stopped had once more begun.